COLLINS

PHRASE BOOK &
DICTIONARY

Spanish

D0681796

HarperCollins*Publishers*

Food section by Edite Vieira Phillips

Other languages in the *Collins Phrase Book & Dictionary* series:

FRENCH
GERMAN
GREEK
ITALIAN
JAPANESE
PORTUGUESE
RUSSIAN

These titles are also published in a language pack containing
60-minute cassette and phrase book

HarperCollins Publishers
P O Box, Glasgow G4 0NB
www.**fire**and**water**.com

First published 1998
Copyright © HarperCollins*Publishers*
Reprint 10 9 8 7 6 5 4
Printed in Italy by Amadeus SpA

ISBN 0 00-472 071 7

INTRODUCTION

Your *Collins Phrase Book & Dictionary* is a handy, quick-reference guide that will help you make the most of your stay abroad. Its clear layout will save you valuable time when you need that crucial word or phrase.

There are three main sections in this book:

Practical topics arranged thematically with an opening section **KEY TALK** containing vital phrases that should stand you in good stead in most situations.

PHRASES

Short easy phrases that can be adapted for your situation

practical tips are highlighted in yellow boxes

SIGNS ARE IN GREEN BOXES

replies you might hear are highlighted in red boxes

FOOD SECTION

Phrases for ordering drinks and food
A region by region description of Spanish food with a note on Spanish wine and other popular drinks
Drinks
Menu reader

DICTIONARY

English-Spanish	Spanish-English	signs highlighted

And finally, a short **GRAMMAR** section explaining how the language works.

So, just flick through the pages to find the information you need. Why not start with a look at pronouncing Spanish on page 6. From there on the going is easy with your *Collins Phrase Book & Dictionary*.

CONTENTS

PRONOUNCING SPANISH

We've tried to make the pronunciation under the phrases as clear as possible. We've broken the words up to make them easy to read, but don't pause between syllables. The syllable to be stressed is shown in **heavy type**. *Spanish isn't really hard to pronounce and once you learn a few basic rules, it shouldn't be too long before you can read straight from the Spanish.*

Most letters are pronounced as in English: **b**, **ch**, **d**, **f**, **k**, **l**, **m**, **n**, **p**, **s**, **t**, **y** *and (usually)* **w** *and* **x**.

As for the vowels, **a** *is always as in* **tap** *(never as in* **tape***);* **e** *is always as in* **pet** *(never as in* **Pete***);* **i** *is always 'ee'; **o** *is always as in* **hop** *(never as in* **hope***);* **u** *is always 'oo' rather than the English sound* **hut**. *They keep their sound even in combination with other letters, so 'au' (eg* **autobus** *ow-to-boos) is like English 'ow', not like English* **automatic**.

The letter **h** *is always silent, and* **r** *is always rolled (even more strongly when double* **r***). Spanish* **v** *and* **b** *are pronounced exactly the same, something like English* **b***, while* **q** *is like English* **k**.

The letter **c** *before* **e** *or* **i** *and the letter* **z** *are pronounced like the* **th** *in thin. The letter* **g** *before* **e** *or* **i** *and the letter* **j** *have the guttural sound you hear in the Scottish word* **loch** *and which we show as* **kh**.

Basic rules to remember are:

spanish	sounds like	example	pronunciation
ll	mi**lli**on	**calle**	*kal-ye*
ñ	o**ni**on	**mañana**	*man-ya-na*
c	**c**at	**comer**	*ko-mer*
c *(before* **e/i***)*	**th**ink	**hacer**	*a-ther*
g	**g**ot	**gafas**	*ga-fas*
g *(before* **e/i***)*	lo**ch**	**hijo**	*ee-kho*
z	**th**ink	**zapatos**	*tha-pa-tos*
j	lo**ch**	**hijo**	*ee-kho*
q	**k**ick	**quiero**	*kyer-o*

Spanish has two forms of address, formal and informal. You should use the informal **tu** only when you know someone well; otherwise use **usted**.

yes	**no**	**that's fine**
sí	no	¡vale!
see	*no*	*ba-le*

please	**thank you**	**de nada**
por favor	gracias	*de **na**-da*
*por fa-**bor***	***grath**-yas*	don't mention it

hello	**goodbye**	**good night**
hola	adiós	buenas noches
***o**-la*	*ad-**yos***	***bwe**-nas **no**-ches*

good morning (until lunch)	**good afternoon/evening** (until dusk)
buenos días	buenas tardes
***bwe**-nos **dee**-yas*	***bwe**-nas **tar**-des*

excuse me!	**sorry!**	**pardon?**
¡oiga por favor!	¡perdón!	¿cómo dice?
oy**-ga por fa-**bor	*per-**don***	***ko**-mo **dee**-the*

Here is an easy way to ask for something... just add **por favor**

a...	**a coffee**	**2 coffees**
un... ('el' words)	un café	dos cafés
oon...	*oon ka-**fe***	*dos ka-**fes***
	a beer	**2 beers**
una... ('la' words)	una cerveza	dos cervezas
***oo**-na...*	***oo**-na ther-**be**-tha*	*dos ther-**be**-thas*

a coffee and two beers, please
un café y dos cervezas, por favor
*oon ka-**fe** ee dos ther-**be**-thas por fa-**bor***

KEY TALK

I'd like...	we'd like...
querÍa...	querÍamos...
ke-**ree**-ya...	ke-**ree**-ya-mos...

I'd like an ice cream
querÍa un helado
ke-**ree**-ya oon e-**la**-do

we'd like to visit Toledo
querÍamos visitar Toledo
ke-**ree**-ya-mos bee-see-**tar** to-**le**-do

| do you have...? |
| ¿tiene...? |
| **tyen**-e... |

do you have any milk?
¿tiene leche?
tyen-e **le**-che

do you have stamps?
¿tiene sellos?
tyen-e **sel**-yos

do you have a map?
¿tiene un mapa?
tyen-e oon **ma**-pa

do you have cheese?
¿tiene queso?
tyen-e **ke**-so

how much is it?	how much does ... cost?
¿cuánto es?	¿cuánto cuesta...?
kwan-to es	**kwan**-to **kwes**-ta

how much is the cheese?
¿cuánto cuesta el queso?
kwan-to **kwes**-ta el **ke**-so

how much is the ticket?
¿cuánto cuesta el billete?
kwan-to **kwes**-ta el beel-**ye**-te

how much is a kilo?
¿cuánto cuesta el quilo?
kwan-to **kwes**-ta el **kee**-lo

how much is it each?
¿cuánto cuesta cada uno?
kwan-to **kwes**-ta **ca**-da **oo**-no

TOMATES...................... 299 KG	TOMATOES PER KILO
PERAS ....499 KG	PEARS PER KILO
NARANJAS ....365 KG	ORANGES PER KILO

where is...?
¿dónde está...?
don-de es-*ta*...

where are...?
¿dónde están...?
don-de es-*tan*...

where is the station?
¿dónde está la estación?
don-de es *ta* la es-tath-*yon*

where are the toilets?
¿dónde están los aseos?
don-de es-*tan* los a-*se*-os

| **SEÑORAS** LADIES | **LIBRE** FREE | **ENTRADA** ENTRANCE |
| **CABALLEROS** GENTS | **OCUPADO** ENGAGED | **SALIDA** EXIT |

is there/are there...?
¿hay...?
a-ee...

is there a restaurant?
¿hay un restaurante?
aee oon rest-ow-*ran*-te

where is there a chemist?
¿dónde hay una farmacia?
don-de aee *oo*-na far-*math* ya

are there children?
¿hay niños?
aee *neen*-yos

is there a swimming pool?
¿hay piscina?
aee pees-*thee*-na

there is no...
no hay...
no aee...

there is no hot water
no hay agua caliente
no aee *ag*-wa kal-*yen*-te

there are no towels
no hay toallas
no aee to-*al*-yas

I need...
necesito...
ne-the-*see*-to...

I need a taxi
necesito un taxi
ne-the-*see*-to oon *tak*-see

I need to send a fax
necesito mandar un fax
ne-the-*see*-to man-*dar* oon faks

KEY TALK

can I...?
¿puedo…?
pwe-do...

can we...?
¿podemos...?
po-*de*-mos...

can I pay?
¿puedo pagar?
pwe-do pa-*gar*

can we go in?
¿podemos entrar?
po-*de*-mos en-trar

where can I...?
¿dónde puedo…?
don-de *pwe*-do...

where can I buy bread?
¿dónde puedo comprar pan?
don-de *pwe*-do kom-*prar* pan

where can I hire bikes?
¿dónde puedo alquilar bicis?
don-de *pwe*-do al-kee-*lar* *bee*-thees

se pueden comprar billetes en el quiosco
*se *pwe*-den kom-*prar* beel-*ye*-tes en el kee-*os*-ko*
you can buy tickets at the kiosk

when?
¿cuándo?
kwan-do

at what time...?
¿a qué hora…?
a ke *o*-ra...

when is breakfast?
¿a qué hora es el desayuno?
a ke *o*-ra es el de-sa-*yoo*-no

when is dinner?
¿a qué hora es la cena?
a ke *o*-ra es la *then*-a

when does it open?
¿cuándo abren?
kwan-do *a*-bren

when does it close?
¿cuándo cierran?
kwan-do *thyerr*-an

yesterday
ayer
a-*yer*

today
hoy
oy

tomorrow
mañana
man-*ya*-na

this morning
esta mañana
es-ta man-*ya*-na

this afternoon
esta tarde
es-ta *tar*-de

tonight
esta noche
es-ta *no*-che

ABIERTO	OPEN
CERRADO	CLOSED
TODOS LOS DÍAS	DAILY
LABORABLES	WEEKDAYS (Mon-Sat)
FESTIVOS	HOLIDAY/SUNDAY

LUN.	MON
MART.	TUE
MIERC.	WED
JUEV.	THU
VIERN.	FRI
SAB.	SAT
DOM.	SUN

is it open?
¿está abierto?
es-ta a-byer-to

is it closed?
¿está cerrado?
es-ta ther-ra-do

2 HORAS 2 HOURS
3 HORAS 3 HOURS

abre a las nueve
ab-re a las nwe-be
it opens at 9

el museo está cerrado los lunes
el moo-se-o es-ta ther-ra-do los loo-nes
the museum is closed on Mondays

GETTING TO KNOW PEOPLE

*The equivalent of Mr is **Señor**, and Mrs or Ms is **Señora**. The word for Miss is **Señorita**, although **Señora** is increasingly used instead.*

how are you?
¿cómo está?
ko-mo es-ta

fine, thanks. And you?
muy bien, gracias. ¿Y usted?
*mooy byen **grath**-yas ee oo-**sted***

my name is...
me llamo...
me lya-mo...

what is your name?
¿cómo se llama?
ko-mo se lya-ma

I don't understand
no entiendo
no en-tyen-do

do you speak English?
¿habla inglés?
a-bla een-gles

MONEY – changing

CAMBIO   BUREAU DE CHANGE
CAJERO AUTOMÁTICO   CASH DISPENSER

*Banks are generally open from 9am-2pm Mon-Fri, and 9am till noon Saturday, except in the summer when they remain closed on Saturdays. Bureaux de change (**Oficina de Cambio**) stay open longer but they charge more in commission than banks.*

where can I change money?
¿dónde se puede cambiar dinero?
*don-de se **pwe**-de kam-**byar** dee-**ne**-ro*

where is the bank?
¿dónde está el banco?
*don-de es-**ta** el **ban**-ko*

where is the bureau de change?
¿dónde está la oficina de cambio?
*don-de es-**ta** la o-fee-**thee**-na de **kam**-byo*

when does the bank open?
¿cuándo abre el banco?
*kwan-do **a**-bre el **ban**-ko*

when does the bank close?
¿cuándo cierra el banco?
*kwan-do **thyerr**-a el **ban**-ko*

I want to cash these traveller's cheques
quiero cambiar estos cheques de viaje
*kyer-o kam-**byar** es-tos **che**-kes de **bya**-khe*

what is the rate?
¿a cómo está el cambio?
*a **ko**-mo es-**ta** el **kam**-byo*

for pounds
de libras
*de **lee**-bras*

for dollars
de dólares
*de do-**la**-res*

I want to change £50
quiero cambiar 50 libras
*kyer-o kam-**byar** theen-**kwen**-ta **lee**-bras*

where is there a cash dispenser?
¿dónde hay un cajero?
*don-de aee oon ka-**khe**-ro*

I'd like small notes
quería billetes pequeños
*ke-**ree**-ya beel-**ye**-tes pe-**ken**-yos*

spending – MONEY

Major credit cards are widely accepted. Usually the card is passed through a reader, but sometimes you have to enter your pin number in a keypad. You can pay in euros using your credit card, but euro notes and coins will not be available until 2002.

how much is it?
¿cuánto es?
kwan-to es

how much will it be?
¿Cuánto me costará?
kwan-to me kos-ta-ra

I want to pay
quiero pagar
kyer-o pa-gar

we want to pay separately
queremos pagar por separado
ke-re-mos pa-gar por se-pa-ra-do

can I pay by credit card?
¿puedo pagar con tarjeta de crédito?
pwe-do pa-gar kon tar-khe-ta de kre-dee-to

I want to pay in euros
quería pagar en euros
ko ree ya en e-oo-ros

do you accept traveller's cheques?
¿aceptan cheques de viaje?
a-thep-tan che-kes de bya-khe

how much is it...?
¿cuánto es...?
kwan-to es...

per person
por persona
por per-so-na

per night
por noche
por no-che

per kilo
por kilo
por kee-lo

are service and VAT included?
¿incluye servicio e IVA?
een-kloo-ye ser-beeth-yo e ee-ba

can I have a receipt?
¿puede darme un recibo?
pwe-de dar-me oon re-theeb-o

do I pay a deposit?
¿tengo que pagar un depósito?
ten-go ke pa-gar oon de-po-see-to

I've nothing smaller
no tengo cambio
no ten-go kam-byo

keep the change
quédese con la vuelta
ke-de-se kon la bwel-ta

AIRPORT

LLEGADAS	ARRIVALS
SALIDAS	DEPARTURES
RECOGIDA DE EQUIPAJE	BAGGAGE RECLAIM
VUELO	FLIGHT
RETRASO	DELAY

to the airport, please
al aeropuerto, por favor
*al aee-ro-**pwer**-to por fa-**bor***

how do I get into town?
¿cómo se va al centro?
***ko**-mo se ba al **then**-tro*

where do I get the bus to the town centre?
¿dónde se coje el autobús para el centro?
***don**-de se **ko**-khe el ow-to-**boos** pa-ra el **then**-tro*

how much is it...?
¿cuánto es...?
***kwan**-to es...*

to the town centre
al centro
*al **then**-tro*

to the airport
al aeropuerto
*al aee-ro-**pwer**-to*

where do I check in for...?
¿dónde se factura para...?
***don**-de se fak-**too**-ra **pa**-ra...*

which gate is it for the flight to...?
¿cuál es la puerta del vuelo para...?
*kwal es la **pwer**-ta del **bwe**-lo **pa**-ra...*

---

el embarque se efectuará en la puerta número...
*el em-**bar**-ke se e-fek-twa-**ra** en la **pwer**-ta **noo**-me-ro...*
boarding will take place at gate number...

última llamada para los pasajeros del vuelo...
***ool**-tee-ma lya-**ma**-da **pa**-ra los pa-sa-**khe**-ros del **bwe**-lo...*
last call for passengers on flight...

su vuelo sale con retraso
*soo **bwe**-lo **sa**-le kon re-**tra**-so*
your flight is delayed

CUSTOMS & PASSPORTS

ADUANA	CUSTOMS
CONTROL DE PASAPORTES	PASSPORT CONTROL
CIUDADANOS UE	EU CITIZENS

With the single European market, EU (European Union) citizens are subject to only highly selective spot checks and they can go through the blue customs channel (unless they have goods to declare). There is no restriction by quantity or value, on goods purchased by travellers in another EU country provided they are for their own personal use (guidelines have been published). If unsure, check with customs officials.

I have nothing to declare
no tengo nada que declarar
*no **ten**-go **na**-da ke de-kla-**rar***

here is...
aqui està...
*a-**kee** es-ta...*

my passport
mi pasaporte
*mee pa-sa-**por**-te*

my green card
mi carta verde
*mee **kar** ta **ber**-de*

do I have to pay duty on this?
¿hay que pagar derechos de aduana por esto?
*aee ke pa-**gar** de **re** chos de a-**dwa**-na por **es**-to*

it's for my own personal use
es para uso personal
*es **pa**-ra **oo**-so per-so-**nal***

we're going to...
vamos a...
***ba**-mos a...*

the children are on this passport
los niños están en este pasaporte
*los **neen**-yos es-**tan** en **es**-te pa-sa-**por**-te*

I'm...
soy...
soy...

English (m/f)
inglés(a)
*een-**gles**(a)*

Australian (m/f)
australiano(a)
*ow-stral-**ya**-no(a)*

15

ASKING THE WAY – questions

excuse me!
¡oiga por favor!
oy-ga por fa-bor

where is...?
¿dónde está...?
don-de es-ta...

where is the nearest...?
¿dónde está el/la ... más próximo(a)?
don-de es-ta el/la ... mas prok-see-mo(a)

how do I get to...?
¿cómo se va a...?
ko-mo se ba a...

is this the right way to...?
¿se va por aquí a...?
se ba por a-kee a...

the...
el/la...
el/la...

is it far?
¿está lejos?
es-ta le-khos

can I walk there?
¿puedo ir andando?
pwe-do eer an-dan-do

is there a bus that goes there?
¿hay algún autobús hasta allí?
aee al-goon ow-to-boos as-ta a-yee

we're looking for...
estamos buscando...
es-ta-mos boos-kan-do...

we're lost
nos hemos perdido
nos e-mos per-dee-do

can you show me on the map?
¿puede indicarme en el mapa?
pwe-de een-dee-kar-me en el ma-pa

answers – ASKING THE WAY

It's no use being able to ask the way if you're not going to understand the directions you get. We've tried to anticipate the likely answers, so listen carefully for these key phrases.

siga todo recto
see-ga to-do rek-to
keep going straight ahead

tiene que dar la vuelta
tyen-e ke dar la bwel-ta
you have to turn round

tuerza... or gire...
twer-tha...or khee-re...
turn...

a la derecha
a la de-re-cha
right

a la izquierda
a la eeth-kyer-da
left

vaya...
ba-ya...
go...

recto
rek-to
straight on

siga
see-ga
keep going straight on

hasta
as-ta
as far as

coja...
ko-kha...
take...

la primera calle a la derecha
la pree-me-ra kal-ye a la de-re-cha
the first on the right

la segunda calle a la izquierda
la se-goon-da kal-ye a la eeth-kyer-da
the second on the left

la carretera de...
la kar-re-te-ra de...
the road to...

siga las señales de...
see-ga las sen-ya-les de...
follow the signs for...

BUS

*Tickets and information on long-distance coach travel are available from travel agents and main bus stations. On local bus journeys you pay on the bus or buy 10 tickets at a time (**un bonobús**) from newspaper kiosks.*

where is the bus station?
¿dónde está la estación de autobuses?
*don-de es-**ta** la es-tath-**yon** de ow-to-**boo**-ses*

I want to go... quiero ir... ***kyer**-o eer...*	**to the station** a la estación *a la es-tath-**yon***	**to the museum** al museo *al moo-**se**-o*
	to the Prado al Prado *al **pra**-do*	**to Toledo** a Toledo *a to-**le**-do*

is there a bus that goes there?
¿hay un autobús que vaya allí?
*aee oon ow-to-**boos** ke **ba**-ya a-**yee***

which bus do I take to go to...?
¿qué autobús se coge para ir a...?
*ke ow-to-**boos** se **ko**-khe **pa**-ra eer a...*

where do I get the bus to...?
¿dónde se coge el autobús para...?
*don-de se **ko**-khe el ow-to-**boos** **pa**-ra...*

how often are the buses? **when is the last bus?**
¿cada cuánto hay autobuses? ¿cuándo sale el último autobús?
*ka-da **kwan**-to aee ow-to-**boos**-es* *kwan-do **sa**-le el **ool**-tee-mo ow-to-**boos***

can you tell me when to get off?
¿me dice cuándo tengo que bajarme?
*me **dee**-the **kwan**-do **ten**-go ke ba-**khar**-me*

18

METRO	UNDERGROUND
ENTRADA	ENTRANCE
SALIDA	EXIT

*Buy your tickets at the underground station. You can also buy a 10-trip ticket (**un bonometro**) which is cheaper than individual tickets and can be used by different people.*

where is the metro station?
¿dónde está la estación de metro?
*don-de es-**ta** la es-tath-**yon** de **me**-tro*

are there any special tourist tickets?
¿hay algún billete de turista?
*aee al-**goon** beel-**ye**-te de too-**rees**-ta*

do you have an underground map?
¿tiene un plano del metro?
***tyen**-e oon **pla**-no del **me**-tro*

I want to go to...
quiero ir a...
***kyer**-o eer a...*

can I go by underground?
¿se puede ir en metro?
*se **pwe**-de eer en **me**-tro*

do I have to change?
¿tengo que cambiar de línea?
***ten**-go ke kam-**byar** de **lee**-ne-a*

where?
¿dónde?
***don**-de*

which line is it for...?
¿qué línea es para ir a...?
*ke **lee**-ne-a es **pa**-ra eer a...*

what is the next stop?
¿cuál es la próxima parada?
*kwal es la **prok**-see-ma pa-**ra**-da*

which is the station for the Prado?
¿cuál es la estación de metro para el Prado?
*kwal es la es-ta-**thyon** de **me**-tro pa-ra el pra-do*

TRAIN

TALGO	INTERCITY EXPRESS
INTERCITY	INTERCITY
DESPACHO DE BILLETES	TICKETS
INFORMACIÓN	INFORMATION
SALIDAS	DEPARTURES
LLEGADAS	ARRIVALS
ANDÉN/VÍA	PLATFORM
CERCANÍAS	LOCAL RAIL NETWORK
COCHE RESTAURANTE	RESTAURANT CAR

*You pay more to travel on the fast intercity services (**TALGO** and **AVE**) and lower rates on the slower trains. Most tickets can be bought from railway stations and travel agents, who will charge a commission. Reduced fares are available on certain days of the year called 'blue days' (**días azules**) – ask at the station for details.*

where is the station?
¿dónde está la estación?
don-de es-ta la es-tath-yon

to the station, please
a la estación, por favor
a la es-tath-yon por fa-bor

a single to...
uno a...
oo-no a...

2 singles to...
dos a...
dos a...

a return to...
uno de ida y vuelta a...
oo-no de ee-da ee bwel-ta a...

2 returns to...
dos de ida y vuelta a...
dos de ee-da ee bwel-ta a...

a child's return to...
un billete de niño, ida y vuelta a...
oon beel-ye-te de neen-yo ee-da ee bwel-ta a...

1st/2nd class
de primera/segunda clase
de pree-me-ra/se-goon-da kla-se

smoking
fumador
foo-ma-dor

non smoking
no fumador
no foo-ma-dor

do I have to pay a supplement?
¿hay que pagar suplemento?
*aee ke pa-**gar** soo-ple-**me**n-to*

is my pass valid on this train?
¿es válido este pase?
*es **ba**-lee-do **es**-te **pa**-se*

I want to book...
quiero reservar...
kyer**-o re-ser-**bar

a seat
un asiento
*oon as-**yen**-to*

a couchette
una litera
***oo** na lee **te** ra*

can I have a timetable?
¿me da un horario?
*me da oon o-**ra**-ree-o*

do I need to change?
¿tengo que hacer transbordo?
***ten** go ke a-**ther** trans-**bor**-do*

where?
¿dónde?
***don**-de*

which platform does it leave from?
¿de qué andén sale?
*de ke an-**den sa**-le*

does the train to ... leave from this platform?
¿el tren para ... sale de este andén?
*el tren **pa**-ra ... **sa** le de **es**-te an-**den***

is this the train for...?
¿es este el tren para...?
*es **es**-te el tren **pa**-ra...*

where is the left-luggage?
¿dónde está la consigna?
***don**-de es-**ta** la kon-**seen**-ya*

is this seat taken?
¿está ocupado?
*es-**ta** o-koo-**pa**-do*

CAR – driving/parking

TODAS DIRECCIONES	ALL ROUTES
SALIDA	EXIT
AUTOPISTA	MOTORWAY
PEAJE	TOLL
PROHIBIDO APARCAR	NO PARKING
CENTRO CUIDAD	CITY CENTRE

*To drive in Spain visitors must have a valid pink EU driver's licence and must be at least 18 years old. When an accident happens the car may be impounded and the driver held in custody pending bail, and for this reason it is advisable to obtain a Bail Bond from your insurer when you get your Green Card. About half of Spanish motorways are toll roads (**autopistas**), the rest are free (**autovías**).*

can I park here?
¿se puede aparcar aquí?
se **pwe**-de a-par-**kar** a-**kee**

where can I park?
¿dónde puedo aparcar?
don-de **pwe**-do a-par-**kar**

is there a car park?
¿hay parking?
aee parking

do I need a parking disc?
¿hace falta tique de aparcamiento?
a-the **fal**-ta **tee**-ke de a-par-ka-**myen**-to

where can I get a parking disc?
¿dónde puedo comprar un tique de aparcamiento?
don-de **pwe**-do kom-**prar** oon **tee**-ke de a-par-ka-**myen**-to

how long can I park here?
¿cuánto tiempo puedo aparcar aquí?
kwan-to **tyem**-po **pwe**-do a-par-**kar** a-**kee**

we're going to...
vamos a...
ba-mos a...

what's the best route?
¿cuál es la mejor ruta?
kwal es la me-**khor** roo-ta

petrol station – CAR

SÚPER	4 STAR
SIN PLOMO	UNLEADED
GASOIL/GASÓLEO	DIESEL
GASOLINA	PETROL
SURTIDOR	PETROL PUMP

If you use a credit card at a motorway service station you will need to show your passport.

is there a petrol station near here?
¿hay alguna gasolinera por aquí?
*aee al-**goo**-na ga-so-lee-**ne**-ra por a-**kee***

fill it up, please
lleno, por favor
lyen**-o por fa-**bor

2000 pesetas worth of 4 star
dos mil pesetas de súper
*dos meel pe-**se**-tas de **soo**-per*

pump number...
surtidor número...
*soor-tee-**dor noo**-me-ro...*

that is my car
ese es mi coche
*e-se es mee **ko**-che*

where is the air line?
¿dónde está el aire?
***don**-de es-**ta** el **aee**-re*

where is the water?
¿dónde está el agua?
***don**-de es-**ta** el **a**-wa*

please check...
¿me revisa...?
*me re-**bee**-sa...*

the tyre pressure
la presión de los neumáticos
*la pres-**yon** de los ne-oo-**ma**-tee-kos*

the oil	**the water**
el aceite	el agua
*el a-**they**-te*	*el **a**-wa*

¿qué surtidor?
*ke soor-tee-**dor***
which pump?

CAR – problems/breakdown

Drivers should carry a first-aid kit, spare light bulbs and a warning triangle for use in the event of an accident or breakdown.

I've broken down
tengo una avería
ten-go **oo**-na a-be-**ree**-ya

what do I do?
¿qué hago?
ke **a**-go

I'm on my own *(female)*
estoy sola
es-**toy so**-la

there are children in the car
hay niños en el coche
aee **neen**-yos en el **ko**-che

where's the nearest garage?
¿dónde está el garaje más próximo?
don-de es-**ta** el ga-**ra**-khe mas **prok**-see-mo

is it serious?
¿es muy serio?
es mooy **ser**-yo

can you repair it?
¿puede arreglarlo?
pwe-de ar-re-**glar**-lo

when will it be ready?
¿para cuándo estará?
pa-ra **kwan**-do es-ta-**ra**

how much will it cost?
¿cuánto me costará?
kwan-to me kos-ta-**ra**

the car won't start
el coche no arranca
el **ko**-che no ar-**ran**-ka

I have a flat tyre
tengo una rueda pinchada
ten-go **oo**-na **rwe**-da peen-**cha**-da

the engine is overheating
el motor se calienta
el mo-**tor** se kal-**yen**-ta

the battery is flat
la batería está descargada
la ba-te-**ree**-ya es-**ta** des-kar-**ga**-da

have you the parts?
¿tiene los repuestos necesarios?
tyen-e los re-**pwes**-tos ne-the-**sar**-yos

it's not working
no funciona
no foon-**thyo**-na

can you replace the windscreen?
¿me puede cambiar el parabrisas?
me **pwe**-de kam-**byar** el pa-ra-**bree**-sas

ALQUILER DE COCHES   CAR HIRE

Cars can be hired at airports and main railway stations, and drivers must be over 21 and hold a valid EU driver's licence.

I want to hire a car
quiero alquilar un coche
kyer-o al-kee-**lar** oon **ko**-che

for one day
para un día
pa-ra oon **dee**-ya

for ... days
para ... días
pa-ra   **dee**-yas

I want...
quiero...
kyer-o...

a large car
un coche grande
oon **ko**-che **gran**-de

an automatic
un automático
oon ow-to-**mat**-ee-ko

a small car
un coche pequeño
oon **ko**-che pe-**ken** yo

how much is it?
¿cúanto es?
kwan-to es

is fully comprehensive insurance included in the price?
¿el seguro a todo riesgo, va incluido en el precio?
el se-**goo**-ro a **to**-do **ryes**-go ba een-kloo-**ee**-do en el **preth**-yo

what do we do if we break down?
¿qué hay que hacer si tenemos una avería?
ke aee ke a-**ther** see te-**ne**-mos **oo**-na a-be-**ree**-ya

when must I return the car by?
¿para qué hora tengo que devolver el coche?
pa-ra ke **o**-ra **ten**-go ke de-bol-**ber** el **ko**-che

please show me the controls
¿me enseña cómo funcionan los mandos?
me en-**sen**-ya **ko**-mo foon-**thyo**-nan los **man**-dos

where are the documents?
¿dónde está la documentación?
don-de es-**ta** la do-koo-men-tath-**yon**

SHOPPING – holiday

ABIERTO	OPEN	**CAJA**	CASH DESK
CERRADO	CLOSED	**REBAJAS**	SALE

Shop opening hours vary but 10am-2pm and 5-8pm Mon-Sat is fairly standard. Food shops open earlier, and large department stores stay open during the lunch hour. Sunday opening is limited: bakeries and newspaper kiosks are open everywhere, but in holiday resorts other shops may open as well.

do you sell...?
¿vende...?
ben-de...

batteries for this camera
pilas para esta cámara
peel-as pa-ra es-ta ka-ma-ra

stamps
sellos
sel-yos

where can I buy...?
¿dónde venden...
don-de ben-den...

stamps
sellos
sel-yos

films
carrete
ka-rre-te

10 stamps
diez sellos
dyeth sel-yos

for postcards
para postales
pa-ra po-sta-les

to Britain
para Gran Bretaña
pa-ra gran bre-tan-ya

a colour film
un carrete en color
oon ka-rre-te en ko-lor

a tape for this video camera
una cinta para esta videocámara
oo-na theen-ta pa-ra es-ta bee-de-o-ka-ma-ra

I'm looking for a present
estoy buscando un regalo
es-toy boos-kan-do oon re-ga-lo

have you anything cheaper?
¿tiene algo más barato?
tyen-e al-go mas ba-ra-to

it's a gift
es un regalo
es oon re-ga-lo

please wrap it up
envuélvamelo por favor
en-bwel-a-me-lo por fa-bor

is there a market?
¿hay mercado?
aee mer-ka-do

when?
¿qué día?
ke dee-ya

clothes – SHOPPING

WOMEN		MEN		SHOES			
UK	EU	UK	EU	UK	EU	UK	EU
8	36	36	46	2	35	7	41
10	38	38	48	3	36	8	42
12	40	40	50	4	37	9	43
14	42	42	52	5	38	10	44
16	44	44	54	6	39	11	45
18	46	46	56	7	41	12	46

can I try this on?
¿puedo probarme esto?
pwe-do pro bar me es-to

it's too big
es demasiado grande
es de-mas-ya-do gran-de

it's too small
es demasiado pequeño
es de-mas-ya-do pe-ken-yo

it's too expensive
es demasiado caro
es de-mas-ya-do ka-ro

I'm just looking
sólo estoy mirando
so-lo es-toy mee-ran-do

I take a size ... shoe
uso el número ... (de zapatos)
oo-so el noo-me-ro ... (de tha-pa-tos)

where are the changing rooms?
¿dónde están los probadores?
don-de es-tan los prob-a-dor-es

have you a smaller size?
¿tiene una talla menor?
tyen-e oo-na tal-ya me-nor

have you a larger size?
¿tiene una talla mayor?
tyen-e oo-na tal-ya ma-yor

I'll take this one
me llevo esto
me lye-bo es-to

¿qué número usa?
ke noo-me-ro oo-sa
what shoe size are you?

¿le queda bien?
le ke-da byen
does it fit?

SHOPPING – food

*You can buy fresh fruit, vegetables and other local produce from the market (**mercado**). Large towns may have a daily market and smaller towns will have one once or twice a week. They are usually open from about 9am to 2pm.*

where can I buy...?	**fruit**	**bread**	**milk**
¿dónde puedo comprar...?	fruta	pan	leche
*don-de **pwe**-do kom-**prar**...*	*froo-ta*	*pan*	*le-che*

where is...?	**supermarket**	**the baker's**
¿dónde está...?	el supermercado	la panadería
*don-de es-**ta**...*	*el soo-per-mer-**ka**-do*	*la pa-na-de-**ree**-ya*

where is the market?	**which day is the market?**
¿dónde está el mercado?	¿qué día hay mercado?
*don-de es-**ta** el mer-**ka**-do*	*ke **dee**-ya aee mer-**ka**-do*

it's me next	**that's enough**
estoy yo ahora	basta
*es-**toy** yo a-**o**-ra*	***bas**-ta*

a litre of...	**milk**	**water**	**beer**
un litro de...	leche	agua	cerveza
*oon **lee**-tro de...*	***le**-che*	***ag**-wa*	*ther-**be**-tha*

a bottle of...	**water**	**wine**	**oil**
una botella de...	agua	vino	aceite
*oo-na bo-**tel**-ya de...*	***ag**-wa*	***bee**-no*	*a-**they**-te*

a can of...	**coke**	**beer**	**tonic water**
una lata de...	coca-cola	cerveza	tónica
*oo-na **la**-ta de...*	*ko-ka-**ko**-la*	*ther-**be**-tha*	***to**-nee-ka*

a carton of...	**orange juice**	**milk**
una caja de...	zumo de naranja	leche
*oo-na **ka**-kha de...*	***thoo**-mo de na-**ran**-kha*	***le**-che*

4 oz of... *(approx.)*
cien gramos de...
*thyen **gra**-mos de...*

cheese
queso
__ke__-so

chorizo
chorizo
cho-__ree__-tho

half a pound of... *(approx.)*
un cuarto kilo de...
*oon **kwar**-to **kee**-lo de...*

sausages
salchichas
*sal-**chee**-chas*

mushrooms
champiñones
*cham-peen-**yo**-nes*

a kilo of...
un kilo de...
*oon **kee**-lo de...*

potatoes
patatas
*pa-**ta**-tas*

apples
manzanas
*man-**tha**-nas*

8 slices of...
ocho lonchas de...
*__o__-cho **lon**-chas de...*

cooked ham
jamón de York
*kha-**mon** de york*

cured ham
jamón serrano
*kha-**mon** ser-**ra**-no*

a loaf of bread
una barra de pan
*__oo__-na **bar**-ra de pan*

three yogurts
tres yogures
*tres yo-**goo**-res*

half a dozen eggs
media docena de huevos
*__med__-ya doth-**en**-a de **we**-bos*

a packet of...
un paquete de...
*oon pa-**ke**-te de...*

biscuits
galletas
*gal-**yet**-as*

sugar
azúcar
*a-**thoo**-kar*

a tin of...
una lata de...
*__oo__-na **la**-ta de...*

tomatoes
tomates
*to-**ma**-tes*

peas
guisantes
*gee-**san**-tes*

a jar of...
un tarro de...
*oon **tar**-ro de...*

jam
mermelada
*mer-me-**la**-da*

olives
aceitunas
*a-they-**too**-nas*

¿qué desea?
ke de-__se__-a
what would you like?

¿algo más?
__al__-go mas
anything else?

SIGHTSEEING

OFICINA DE TURISMO   TOURIST OFFICE

Tourist offices will provide town plans, information on accommodation, restaurants and local attractions.

where is the tourist office?
¿dónde está la oficina de turismo?
don-de es-*ta* la o-fee-*thee*-na de too-*rees*-mo

we'd like to visit...
queríamos visitar...
ke-ree-ya-mos bee-see-*tar*...

have you any leaflets?
¿tiene algún folleto?
tyen-e al-*goon* fol-*ye*-to

when can we visit...?
¿cuándo se puede visitar...?
kwan-do se *pwe*-de bee-see-*tar*...

do you have a town guide?
¿tiene una guía de la cuidad?
tyen-e *oo*-na *gee*-ya de la thyoo-*dad*

what day does it close?
¿qué día cierra?
ke *dee*-ya *thyerr*-a

is it open to the public?
¿está abierto al público?
es-*ta* ab-*yer*-to al *poob*-lee-ko

we'd like to go to...
queríamos ir a...
ke-*ree*-ya-mos eer a...

are there any excursions?
¿hay alguna excursión organizada?
*a*ee al-*goo*-na eks-koor-*syon* or-ga-nee-*tha*-da

when does it leave?
¿a qué hora sale?
a ke *o*-ra *sa*-le

where does it leave from?
¿de dónde sale?
de *don*-de *sa*-le

how much is it to get in?
¿cúanto cuesta entrar?
kwan-to *kwes*-ta en-*trar*

is there a reduction for...?
¿hay descuento para...?
*a*ee des-*kwen*-to *pa*-ra...

children
niños
neen-yos

students
estudiantes
e-stoo-*dyan*-tes

unemployed
parados
pa-*ra*-dos

senior citizens
jubilados
khoo-bee-*la*-dos

32

BEACH

PROHIBIDO BAÑARSE	NO SWIMMING
PROHIBIDO TIRARSE	NO DIVING
PELIGRO	DANGER

A green flag flying at the beach means it is safe to go swimming, a yellow flag means you can swim, but it is not recommended, and red flag means it is dangerous. Beaches which meet European standards of cleanliness are allowed to fly a blue flag. Watersports are popular in Spain and you can hire boats and sailboards at some resorts.

which is a quiet beach?
¿hay alguna playa tranquila?
*aee al-**goo**-na **pla**-ya tran-**kee**-la*

is there a swimming pool?
¿hay piscina?
*aee pees-**thee**-na*

can we swim in the river?
¿podemos bañarnos en el río?
*po-**de**-mos ban-**yar** nos en el **ree**-yo*

is the water deep?
¿es muy profundo?
*es mooy pro-**foon**-do*

is it dangerous?
¿es peligroso?
*es pe-lee-**gro**-so*

how do I get there?
¿cómo se va hasta allí?
*ko-mo se ba **as**-ta a-**yee***

is the water clean?
¿está limpia el agua?
*es-**ta** leem-pya el **ag**-wa*

is the water cold?
¿está fría el agua?
*es-**ta** free-ya el **ag**-wa*

are there currents?
¿hay corrientes?
*aee korr-**yen**-tes*

where can we...?
¿dónde se puede...?
*don-de se **pwe**-de...*

can I hire...?
¿puedo alquilar...?
***pwe**-do al-kee-**lar**...*

windsurf
hacer surfing
*a-**ther** soor-**feeng***

a beach umbrella
una sombrilla
***oo**-na som-**breel**-ya*

waterski
hacer esquí acuático
*a-**ther** e-**skee** a-**kwa**-tee-ko*

a jetski
una moto acuática
***oo**-na **mo**-to ak-**wa**-tee-ka*

SPORT

Tourist offices will provide information on sports activities in their area.

where can we...?
¿dónde se puede...?
don-de se pwe-de...

play tennis
jugar al tenis
khoo-gar al te-nees

play golf
jugar al golf
khoo-gar al golf

go swimming
nadar
na-dar

hire bikes
alquilar bicis
al-kee-lar bee-thees

go fishing
ir a pescar
eer a pes-kar

go riding
montar a caballo
mon-tar a ka-bal-yo

how much is it...?
¿cuánto cuesta...?
kwan-to kwes-ta...

per hour
por hora
por o-ra

per day
por día
por dee-ya

how do I book a court?
¿cómo se reserva una pista?
ko-mo se re-ser-ba oo-na pee-sta

can I hire rackets?
¿puedo alquilar raquetas?
pwe-do al-kee-lar ra-ke-tas

do I need a fishing permit?
hace falta licencia de pesca?
a-the fal-ta lee-thenth-ya de pes-ka

where can I get one?
¿dónde puedo conseguir una?
don-de pwe-do kon-se-geer oo-na

is there a football match?
¿hay algún partido de fútbol?
aee al-goon par-tee-do de foot-bol

do I need walking boots?
¿necesito botas de montaña?
ne-the-see-to bo-tas de mon-tan-ya

where is there a sports shop?
¿dónde hay una tienda de deportes?
don-de aee oo-na tyen-da de de-por-tes

There are good skiing facilities in the Sierra Nevada and Catalonia.

can I hire skis?
¿puedo alquilar unos esquíes?
pwe-do al-kee-lar oo-nos es-kee-es

how much is a pass?
¿cuánto cuesta un forfait?
kwan-to kwes-ta oon for-faeet

I'm a beginner
soy principiante
soy preen-theep-ee-an-te

which is an easy run?
¿hay alguna pista facil?
aee al-goo-na pee-sta fa-theel

what is the snow like today?
¿cómo está la nieve hoy?
ko-mo es-ta la nyeb-e oy

is there a map of the ski runs?
¿hay un mapa de pistas?
aee oon ma-pa de pee-stas

my skis are...	**too long**	**too short**
mis esquíes son...	demasiado largos	demasiado cortos
mees es-kee-es son...	*de mas ya-do lar-gos*	*de-mas-ya-do kor-tos*

my bindings are...	**too loose**	**very tight**
tengo las fijaciones...	demasiado flojas	muy prietas
ten-go las fee-khath-yon-es...	*de-mas-ya-do flo-khas*	*mooy pryet-as*

where can we go cross-country skiing?
¿dónde se puede hacer esquí de fondo?
don-de se pwe-de a-ther es-kee de fon-do

¿de qué largura quiere los esquíes?
de ke lar-goo-ra kyer-e los es-kee-es
what length skis do you want?

¿qué número de zapato usa?
ke noo-me-ro de tha-pa-to oo-sa
what is your shoe size?

NIGHTLIFE – popular

Spanish people tend to dine late and then go out afterwards. An evening out might not start until 10pm and typically involves visiting a series of bars, staying for only a short time in each one.

what is there to do at night?
¿qué se puede hacer por las noches?
*ke se **pwe**-de a-**ther** por las **no**-ches*

which is a good bar?
¿qué bares buenos hay?
*ke **ba**-res **bwe**-nos aee*

which is a good disco?
¿qué discotecas buenas hay?
*ke dees-ko-te-kas **bwe**-nas aee*

where can we hear live music?
¿dónde hay música en vivo?
***don**-de aee **moo**-see-ka en **bee**-bo*

is it expensive?
¿es caro?
*es **ka**-ro*

where can we hear flamenco/salsa?
¿dónde se puede escuchar flamenco/salsa?
***don**-de se **pwe**-de es-koo-**char** fla-**men**-ko/**sal**-sa*

where do local people go at night?
¿dónde va la gente de aquí por la noche?
***don**-de ba la **khen**-te de a-**kee** por la **no**-che*

is it a safe area?
¿es una zona segura?
*es **oo**-na **tho**-na se-**goo**-ra*

are there any concerts?
¿hay algún concierto?
*aee al-**goon** kon-thyer-to*

¿quieres bailar?
kyer**-es baee-**lar
do you want to dance?

me llamo...
*me **lya**-mo...*
my name is...

¿cómo te llamas?
***ko**-mo te **lya**-mas*
what's your name?

36

Museums are usually closed on Mondays. Opening hours vary but it is normal for museums to open from 10am to 2pm and sometimes to reopen in the early evening from 5 to 8pm. There are many drama, dance and music summer festivals – they begin generally late at night, about 10.30 or 11pm.

is there a list of cultural events?
¿hay alguna guía del ocio?
*aee al-**goo**-na **gee**-ya del **oth**-yo*

when is the local festival?
¿cuándo son las fiestas de aquí?
kwan**-do son las **fyes**-tas de a-**kee

we'd like to go...
queríamos ir...
*ke-**ree**-ya-mos eer...*

to the theatre
al teatro
*al te-**a**-tro*

to the opera
a la ópera
*a la **o**-pe-ra*

to the ballet
al ballet
*al ba-**le***

to a concert
a un concierto
*a oon kon-**thyer**-to*

what's on?
¿qué ponen?
*ke **po**-nen*

do I need to get tickets in advance?
¿tengo que sacar las entradas antes?
***ten**-go ke sa-**kar** las en-**trad**-es **an**-tes*

how much are the tickets?
¿cuánto cuestan las entradas?
***kwan**-to **kwes**-tan las en-**tra**-das*

when does the performance end?
¿cuándo termina la representación?
kwan**-do ter-**mee**-na la re-pre-sen-tath-**yon

2 tickets...
dos entradas...
*dos en-**tra**-das...*

for tonight
para esta noche
***pa**-ra **es**-ta **no**-che*

for tomorrow
para mañana
***pa**-ra man-**ya**-na*

for 5th August
para el cinco de agosto
***pa**-ra el **theen**-ko de a-**gos**-to*

HOTEL

Tourist offices have lists of hotels and other accommodation in their areas. You might also want to treat yourself to a stay in a **parador** *– luxurious state-run hotels which are often converted palaces, monasteries or other historic buildings.*

have you a room for tonight?
¿tiene una habitación para esta noche?
tyen-e **oo**-na a-bee-tath-**yon** pa-ra **es**-ta **no**-che

a room	**single**	**double**	**family**
una habitación	individual	doble	familiar
oo-na a-bee-tath-**yon**	een-dee-bee-**dwal**	**dob**-le	fa-meel-**yar**
	with a shower	**with a bath**	
	con ducha	con baño	
	kon **doo**-cha	kon **ban**-yo	

how much is it per night?
¿cuánto cuesta por noche?
kwan-to **kwes**-ta por **no**-che

is breakfast included?
¿es con desayuno?
es kon de-sa-**yoo**-no

I booked a room
tengo reservada una habitación
ten-go re-ser-**ba**-da **oo**-na a-bee-tath-**yon**

my name is...
soy...
soy...

I'd like to see the room
quería ver la habitación
ke-**ree**-ya ber la a-bee-tath-**yon**

have you anything cheaper?
¿tiene algo más barato?
tyen-e **al**-go mas ba-**ra**-to

I want a room with three beds
quiero una habitación con tres camas
kyer-o **oo**-na a-bee-tath-**yon** kon tres **ka**-mas

can I leave this in the safe?
¿puedo dejar esto en la caja fuerte?
pwe-do de-**khar es**-to en la **ka**-kha **fwer**-te

38

can I have my key, please?
¿puede darme la llave, por favor?
pwe-de dar-me la lya-be por fa-bor

are there any messages for me?
¿hay algún mensaje para mí?
aee al-goon men-sa-khe pa-ra mee

come in!
¡pase!
pa-se

please come back later
por favor, vuelva más tarde
por fa-bor bwel-ba mas tar-de

I'd like breakfast in my room
quería desayunar en la habitación
ker-ee-ya de-sa-yoo-nar en la a-bee-tath-yon

please bring...
¿me trae, por favor...?
me tra-ye por fa-bor...

toilet paper
papel higiénico
pa-pel eekh-yen-ee-ko

soap
jabón
kha-bon

clean towels
toallas limpias
twal-yas leemp-yas

a glass
un vaso
oon ba-so

could you clean...?
¿puede limpiar...?
pwe-de leem-pyar

my room
la habitación
la a-bee-tath-yon

the bath
el baño
el ban-yo

please call me...
por favor, despiérteme...
por fa-bor des-pyer-te-me...

at 8 o'clock
a las ocho
a las o-cho

do you have a laundry service?
¿tienen servicio de lavandería?
tyen-en ser-beeth-yo de la-ban-de-ree-a

we're leaving tomorrow
nos vamos mañana
nos ba-mos man-ya-na

please prepare the bill
¿me hace la factura, por favor?
me a-the la fak-too-ra fa-bor

SELF-CATERING

The voltage in Spain is 220, but some older buildings may still use 125 volts. Plugs have two round pins and you should take an adaptor if you plan to take any electrical appliances with you.

which is the key for this door?
¿cuál es la llave de esta puerta?
*kwal es la **lya**-be de **es**-ta **pwer**-ta*

please show us how this works
enséñenos cómo funciona esto, por favor
*es-**sen**-ye-nos **ko**-mo foonth-**yon**-a **es**-to por fa-**bor***

how does ... work?
¿cómo funciona...?
***ko**-mo foonth-**yon**-a...*

the waterheater
el calentador del agua
*el ka-len-ta-**dor** del **a**-wa*

the washing machine
la lavadora
*la la-ba-**dor**-a*

the cooker
la cocina
*la ko-**thee**-na*

who do I contact if there are any problems?
¿a quién aviso si hay algún problema?
*a kyen a-**bee**-so see aee al-**goon** prob-**le**-ma*

we need extra...
nos hacen falta más...
*nos **a**-then **fal**-ta mas...*

cutlery
cubiertos
*koo-**yer**-tos*

sheets
sábanas
***sab**-a-nas*

the gas has run out
se ha acabado el gas
*se a a-ka-**ba**-do el gas*

what do I do?
¿qué hago?
*ke **a**-go*

where are the fuses?
¿dónde están los fusibles?
***don**-de es-**tan** los foo-**seeb**-les*

where do I put the rubbish?
¿dónde se deja la basura?
***don**-de se **de**-kha la ba-**soo**-ra*

CAMPING & CARAVANNING

When camping in Spain you must use an approved site. There are many sites along the coast, fewer in the inland areas; all are classified according to the facilities they provide. A car towing a caravan or trailer must not exceed 50 kph in built-up areas, and 70 or 80 kph on other roads.

we're looking for a campsite
estamos buscando un camping
*es-**ta**-mos boos-**kan**-do oon **kam**-peen*

have you a list of campsites?
¿tiene una guía de campings?
*tyen-e **oo**-na **gee**-ya de **kam**-peen*

where is the campsite?
¿dónde está el camping?
***don**-de es-**ta** el **kam**-peen*

have you any vacancies?
¿tienen sitio?
***tyen**-en **seet**-yo*

how much is it per night?
¿cuánto cuesta por noche?
***kwan**-to **kwes**-ta por **no**-che*

we'd like to stay for ... nights
queríamos quedarnos ... noches
*ke-**ree**-ya-mos ke-**dar**-nos ... **no**-ches*

is the campsite near the beach?
¿está el camping cerca de la playa?
*es-**ta** el **kam**-peen **ther**-ka de la **pla**-ya*

do you have a more sheltered site?
¿tienen algún sitio más resguardado?
***tyen**-en al-**goon see**-tyo mas res-gwar-**da**-do*

it is very muddy here
aquí hay mucho barro
*a-**kee** aee **moo**-cho **bar**-ro*

is there another site?
¿hay otro sitio?
*aee **o**-tro **see**-tyo*

is there a shop on the site?
¿hay alguna tienda en el camping?
*aee al-**goo**-na **tyen**-da en el **kam**-peen*

can we camp here?
¿podemos acampar aquí?
*po-**de**-mos a-kam-**par** a-**kee***

can we park our caravan here?
¿podemos aparcar la caravana aquí?
*po-**de**-mos a-par-**kar** la ka-ra-**ba**-na a-**kee***

for the night
por esta noche
*por **es**-ta **no**-che*

CHILDREN

Children under 12 are not allowed to travel in the front seat of cars unless they use a suitable restraint system.

a child's ticket *(for transport)*
un billete de niño
oon beel-ye-te de neen-yo

(for entertainment)
una entrada de niño
oo-na en-tra-da de neen-yo

is there a reduction for children?
¿hay descuento para niños?
aee des-kwen-to pa-ra neen-yos

do you have a children's menu?
¿tienen menú para niños?
tyen-e me-noo pa-ra neen-yos

do you have...?
¿tiene...?
tyen-e...

a high chair
una silla alta
oo-na seel-ya al-ta

a cot
una cuna
oo-na koo-na

is it ok to bring children here?
¿pueden entrar los niños aquí?
pwe-den en-trar los neen-yos a-kee

what is there for children to do?
¿qué cosas hay para los niños?
ke ko-sas aee pa-ra los neen-yos

is it safe for children?
¿es seguro para los niños?
es se-goo-ro pa-ra los neen-yos

is it dangerous?
¿es peligroso?
es pe-lee-gro-so

I have two children
tengo dos hijos
ten go dos ee-khos

he/she is 10 years old
tiene diez años
tyen-e dyeth an-yos

do you have children?
¿tiene hijos?
tyen-e ee-khos

SPECIAL NEEDS

Tourist offices provide information on provision in their areas.
Some youth hostels and a few hotels have facilities for disabled
travellers.

is it possible to visit ... with a wheelchair?
¿se puede entrar en ... con silla de ruedas?
se pwe-de en-trar en ... kon seel-ya de rwed-as

do you have toilets for the disabled?
¿hay aseos para minusválidos?
aee a-se-os pa-ra mee-noos-ba-lee-dos

I need a bedroom on the ground floor
necesito una habitación en la planta baja
ne-the-see-to oo-na a-bee-tath-yon en la plan-ta ba-kha

is there a lift?	**where is the lift?**
¿hay ascensor?	¿dónde está el ascensor?
aee as-then-sor	*don-de es-ta el as-then-sor*

I can't walk far
no puedo andar mucho
no pwe-do an-dar moo-cho

are there many steps?
¿hay muchos escalones?
aee moo-chos es-ka-lo-nes

is there an entrance for wheelchairs?
¿hay acceso para sillas de ruedas?
aee ak-the-so pa-ra seel-yas de rwed-as

can I travel on this train with a wheelchair?
¿puedo viajar en este tren con silla de ruedas?
pwe-do bya-khar en es-te tren kon seel-ya de rwed-as

is there a reduction for the disabled?
¿hay descuento para minusválidos?
aee des-kwen-to pa-ra mee-noos-ba-lee-dos

EXCHANGE VISITORS

These phrases are intended for families hosting Spanish-speaking visitors. We have used the familiar **tu** form.

what would you like for breakfast?
¿qué quieres de desayuno?
*ke **kyer**-es de de-sa-**yoo**-no*

do you eat...?
¿comes...?
ko-mes...

what would you like to eat?
¿qué quieres de comer
*ke **kyer**-es de ko-**mer***

what would you like to drink?
¿qué quieres de beber?
*ke **kyer**-es de be-**ber***

did you sleep well?
¿has dormido bien?
*as dor-**mee**-do byen*

would you like to take a shower?
¿quieres darte una ducha?
***kyer**-es **dar**-te **oo**-na **doo**-cha*

what would you like to do today?
¿qué quieres hacer hoy?
*ke **kyer**-es a-**ther** oy*

would you like to go shopping?
¿quieres ir de compras?
***kyer**-es eer de **kom**-pras*

I will pick you up at...
te iré a recoger a...
*te ee-**re** a re-ko-**kher** a...*

did you enjoy yourself?
¿te lo has pasado bien?
*te lo as pa-**sa**-do byen*

take care
ten cuidado
*ten kwee-**da**-do*

please be back by...
vuelve antes de...
***bwel**-be **an**-tes de...*

we'll be in bed when you get back
cuando vuelvas estaremos en la cama
***kwan**-do **bwel**-bas es-ta-**re**-mos en la **ka**-ma*

EXCHANGE VISITORS

These phrases are intended for those people staying with Spanish-speaking families.

I like...
me gusta...
*me **goo**-sta...*

I don't like...
no me gusta...
*no me **goo**-sta...*

that was delicious
estaba buenísimo
*es-**ta**-ba bwe-**nee**-see-mo*

thank you very much
muchas gracias
*moo-chas **grath**-yas*

may I phone home?
¿puedo llamar a casa?
*pwe-do lya-**mar** a **ka**-sa*

may I make a local call?
¿puedo hacer una llamada local?
*pwe-do a-**ther** oo-na lya-**ma**-da lo-**kal***

can I have a key?
¿me deja una llave?
*me **de**-kha oo-na **lya**-be*

can you take me by car?
¿puede llevarme en coche?
*pwe-de lye-**bar**-me en **ko**-che*

can I borrow...?
¿me deja...?
*me **de**-kha...*

an iron
una plancha
*oo-na **plan**-cha*

a hairdryer
un secador
*oon se-ka-**dor***

what time do you get up?
¿a qué hora se levanta?
*a ke **o**-ra se le-**ban**-ta*

please would you call me at...
¿me puede llamar a las...?
*me **pwe**-de lya-**mar** a las...*

who are you staying with?
¿con quién te quedas?
*kon kyen te **ke**-das*

I'm staying with...
me quedo con...
*me **ke**-do kon...*

how long are you staying?
¿cuánto tiempo te vas a quedar?
*kwan-to **tyem**-po te bas a ke-**dar***

I'm leaving in a week
me voy dentro de una semana
*me **boy** den-tro de oo-na se-**ma**-na*

thanks for everything
gracias por todo
***grath**-yas por **to**-do*

I've had a great time
lo he pasado muy bien
*lo e pa-**sa**-do mooy byen*

PROBLEMS

can you help me, please?
¿puede ayudarme, por favor?
pwe-de a-yoo-*dar*-me por fa-*bor*

I don't speak Spanish
no hablo español
no *ab*-lo es-pan-*yol*

do you speak English?
¿habla inglés?
ab-la een-*gles*

does anyone speak English?
¿hay alguien que hable inglés?
aee *al*-gyen ke *ab*-le een-*gles*

I'm lost
me he perdido
me e per-*dee*-do

how do I get to...?
¿cómo voy a...?
ko-mo boy a...

I'm late
llego tarde
lyeg-o *tar*-de

I need to get to...
tengo que ir a...
ten-go ke eer a...

I've missed...
he perdido...
e per-*dee*-do...

my plane
el vuelo
el *bwe*-lo

my connection
el enlace
el en-*lath*-e

I've lost...
he perdido...
e per-*dee*-do...

my wallet
la cartera
la kar-*te*-ra

my passport
el pasaporte
el pa-sa-*por*-te

my luggage has not arrived
no ha llegado mi equipaje
no a *lyeg*-a-do mee e-kee-*pa*-khe

I've left my bag in...
me he dejado la bolsa en...
me e de-*kha*-do la *bol*-sa en...

on the coach
en el autocar
en el ow-to-*kar*

is there a lost property office?
¿hay una oficina de objetos perdidos?
aee *oo*-na o-fee-*thee*-na de ob-*khe*-tos per-*dee*-dos

leave me alone!
¡déjeme en paz!
de-khe-me en path

go away!
¡váyase!
ba-ya-se

COMPLAINTS

the light
la luz
la looth

the air conditioning
el aire acondicionado
el aee-re a-kon-deeth-yon-a-do

...doesn't work
...no funciona
...no toonth-yon-a

the room is dirty
la habitación está sucia
la a-bee-tath-yon es-ta sooth-ya

the bath is dirty
el baño está sucio
el ban-yo es ta sooth-yo

there is no...
no hay...
no aee...

hot water
agua caliente
ag-wa kal-yen-te

toilet paper
papel higiénico
pa-pel eekh-yen-ee-ko

it is too noisy
hay demasiado ruido
aee de-mas-ya-do rwee-do

it is too small
es demasiado pequeño
es de-mas-ya-do pe-ken-yo

this isn't what I ordered
esto no es lo que he pedido
es-to no es lo ke e pe-dee-do

I want to complain
quiero hacer una reclamación
kyer-o a-ther oo-na re-kla-math-yon

I want my money back
quiero que me devuelvan el dinero
kyer-o ke me de-bwel-ban el dee-ne-ro

we've been waiting for a very long time
llevamos mucho tiempo esperando
lyeb-a-mos moo-cho tyem-po es-pe-ran-do

there is a mistake
hay un error
aee oon er-ror

this is broken
esto está roto
es-to es-ta ro-to

can you repair it?
¿puede arreglarlo?
pwe-de ar-reg-lar-lo

EMERGENCIES

POLICÍA	POLICE
BOMBEROS	FIRE BRIGADE
URGENCIAS	CASUALTY DEPARTMENT

POLICE (nationwide)	091
AMBULANCE	call the police and they will make arrangements
FIRE (Madrid, Barcelona and Seville)	080
FIRE (elsewhere)	check with the operator

help!
¡socorro!
so-**kor**-ro

can you help me?
¿me puede ayudar?
me **pwe**-de a-yoo-**dar**

there's been an accident
ha habido un accidente
a a-**bee**-do oon ak-thee-**den**-te

someone is injured
hay un herido
aee oon er-**ee**-do

call...
llame a...
lya-me a...

the police
la policía
la po-lee-**thee**-ya

an ambulance
una ambulancia
oo-na am-boo-**lan**-thya

he was driving too fast
él iba demasiado rápido
el **ee**-ba de-mas-**ya**-do **rap**-ee-do

where's the police station?
¿dónde está la comisaría?
don-de es-**ta** la kom-ee-sa-**ree**-ya

the insurance company requires me to report it
la compañía de seguros me exige que lo notifique
la kom-pan-**yee**-ya de se-**goo**-ros me ek-**see**-khe ke lo no-tee-**fee**-ke

I've been robbed
me han robado
*me an ro-**ba**-do*

I've been attacked
me han agredido
*me an ag-re-**dee**-do*

I've been raped
me han violado
*me an byo-**la**-do*

my car has been broken into
me han entrado en el coche
*me an en-**tra**-do en el **ko**-che*

my car has been stolen
me han robado el coche
*me an ro-**ba**-do el **ko**-che*

that man keeps following me
ese hombre me está siguiendo
*e-se **om**-bre me es-**ta** seeg-**yen**-do*

how much is the fine?
¿cuánto es la multa?
***kwan**-to es la **mool**-ta*

I don't have enough
no tengo suficiente
*no **ten**-go soo-fee-**thyen**-te*

can I pay at the police station?
¿puedo pagar en la comisaría?
***pwe**-do pa-**gar** en la ko-mee-sa-**ree**-ya*

I would like to phone my embassy
quería llamar a mi embajada
*ke-**ree**-ya lya-**mar** a mee em-ba-**kha**-da*

where is the British Consulate?
¿dónde está el consulado británico?
***don**-de es-**ta** el kon-soo-**la**-do bree-**tan**-ee-ko*

I have no money
no tengo dinero
*no **ten**-go dee-**ne**-ro*

vamos para allá
ba**-mos **pa**-ra al-**ya
we are on our way

HEALTH

FARMACIA	PHARMACY
HOSPITAL	HOSPITAL
URGENCIAS	ACCIDENT AND EMERGENCY DEPT

EU citizens are entitled to free emergency care in Spain. You should take with you form E111, completed and stamped at a post office in the UK before your trip. However you will need to take out a medical insurance policy to cover non-emergency treatment. Pharmacies will be able to provide advice on any health matters and deal with minor problems.

have you something for...?
¿tiene algo para...
tyen-e al-go pa-ra...

car sickness
el mareo
el ma-re-o

diarrhoea
la diarrea
la dee-ar-re-a

is it safe for children to take?
¿lo pueden tomar los niños?
lo pwe-den to-mar los neen-yos

I don't feel well
me encuentro mal
me en-kwen-tro mal

I need a doctor
necesito un médico
ne-the-see-to oon med-ee-ko

my son/daughter is ill
mi hijo/hija está enfermo(a)
mee ee-kho/ee-kha es-ta en-fer-mo(a)

he/she has a temperature
tiene fiebre
tyen-e fyeb-re

I'm taking these drugs
estoy tomando estos medicamentos
es-toy to-man-do es-tos me-dee-ka-men-tos

I have high blood pressure
tengo la tensión alta
ten-go la ten-syon al-ta

I'm pregnant
estoy embarazada
es-toy em-ba-ra-tha-da

I'm on the pill
estoy tomando la píldora
es-toy tom-an-do la peel-do-ra

I'm allergic to penicillin
soy alérgico(a) a la penicilina
soy a-**ler**-khee-ko(a) a la pen-ce-thee-**lee**-na

my blood group is...
mi grupo sanguíneo es...
mee **groo**-po san-**gee**-ne-o es...

I'm breastfeeding
estoy dando de mamar
es-**toy dan**-do de ma-**mar**

is it safe to take?
¿tiene contraindicaciones?
tyen-e con-tra-een-dee-kath-**yon**-es

will he/she have to go to hospital?
¿tendrá que ir al hospital?
ten-**dra** ke eer al os-pee-**tal**

I need to go to casualty
tengo que ir a urgencias
ten-go ke eer a oor-**khenth**-yas

where is the hospital?
¿dónde está el hospital?
don-de es **ta** el os-pee **tal**

when are visiting hours?
¿cuáles son las horas de visita?
kwal-es son las **o**-ras de bee-**see**-ta

which ward?
¿qué planta?
ke **plan**-ta

I need to see the dentist
necesito ver al dentista
ne-the-**see**-to ber al den-**tees**-ta

I have toothache
me duele una muela
me **dwe**-le **oo**-na **mwe**-la

the filling has come out
se me ha caído el empaste
se me a ka-**ee**-do el em-**pas**-te

it hurts
me duele
me **dwe**-le

my dentures are broken
se me ha roto la dentadura postiza
se me a **ro**-to la den-ta-**doo**-ra pos-**tee**-tha

can you repair them?
¿puede arreglarla?
pwe-de ar-reg-**lar**-la

I have an abscess
tengo un absceso
ten-go oon ab-**thes**-o

BUSINESS

Office hours vary but most offices open at 9am, take a long lunch hour (usually from 1 or 2pm till 4 or 5pm) and close at 7 or 8 in the evening. Government offices are open to the public from 9am to 2pm.

I'm...
soy...
soy...

here's my card
aquí tiene mi tarjeta
*a-**kee tyen**-e mee tar-**khe**-ta*

I'm from Jones Ltd
soy de la empresa Jones
*soy de la em-**pre**-sa Jones*

I'd like to arrange a meeting with Mr/Ms...
quería tener una reunión con el señor/la señora...
*ke-**ree**-ya te-**ner** oo-na re-oon-**yon** kon el sen-**yor**/la sen-**yor**-a...*

can we meet at a restaurant?
¿podemos vernos en un restaurante?
*po-**de**-mos **ber**-nos en oon rest-ow-**ran**-te*

I will send a fax to confirm
se lo confirmaré por fax
*se lo kon-feer-ma-**re** por faks*

I'm staying at Hotel...
estoy en el Hotel...
*es-**toy** en el o-**tel**...*

how do I get to your office?
¿cómo se va a su oficina?
***ko**-mo se ba a soo o-fee-**thee**-na*

here is some information about my company
aquí tiene información sobre mi empresa
*a-**kee tyen**-e een-for-math-**yon sob**-re mee em-**pre**-sa*

BUSINESS

I have an appointment with...
tengo una cita con...
ten-go oo-na thee-ta kon...

at ... o'clock
a las...
a las...

I'm delighted to meet you
¡encantado(a) de conocerle!
en kan ta-do(a) de ko-no-ther-le

my Spanish isn't very good
no hablo muy bien español
no ab-lo mooy byen es-pan-yol

what is the name of the managing director?
¿cómo se llama el director gerente?
ko-mo se lya-ma el dee-rek-tor khe-ren-te

I would like some information about the company
quería información sobre la empresa
ke-ree-ya een-for-math-yon sob-re la em-pre-sa

do you have a press office?
¿tiene oficina de prensa?
tyen-e o-fee-thee-na de pren-sa

I need an interpreter
necesito un intérprete
ne-the-see-to oon een-ter-pre-te

can you photocopy this for me?
¿me puede fotocopiar esto?
me pwe-de fo-to-kop-yar es-to

is there a business centre?
¿hay algún centro de negocios?
aee al-goon then-tro de ne-go-thyos

está usted citado(a)?
es-ta oo-sted thee-ta-do(a)
do you have an appointment?

PHONING

Coin-operated payphones take 25- and 100-peseta coins, but
card-operated machines are becoming much more common –
you can buy phonecards from newsstands and tobacconists
(**estancos**). International calls are relatively expensive. To call
abroad, dial 07 before the country code, which for the UK is 44.

a phonecard
una tarjeta telefónica
*oo-na tar-**khe**-ta te-le-**fo**-nee-ka*

for 1000/for 2000 pesetas
de mil/de dos mil pesetas
*de meel/de dos meel pe-**se**-tas*

I want to make a phone call
quiero hacer una llamada
***kyer**-o a-**ther oo**-na lya-**ma**-da*

I want to make a reverse charge call
quiero hacer una llamada a cobro revertido
***kyer**-o a-**ther oo**-na lya-**ma**-da a **ko**-bro re-ber-**tee**-do*

can I speak to...?
¿puedo hablar con...?
***pwe**-do a-**blar** kon...*

this is...
soy...
soy...

Señor Rugama, please
con el señor Rugama, por favor
*kon el sen-**yor** roo-**ga**-ma por fa-**bor***

I'll call back later
le volveré a llamar más tarde
*le bol-be-**re** a lya-**mar** mas **tar**-de*

can you give me an outside line, please
¿me da línea, por favor?
*me da **lee**-ne-a por fa-**bor***

diga
***dee**-ga*
hello

¿de parte de quién?
*de **par**-te de kyen*
who is calling?

está comunicando
*es-**ta** ko-moo-nee-**kan**-do*
it's engaged

¿puede volver a llamar más tarde?
***pwe**-de bol-**ber** a lya-**mar** mas **tar**-de*
please try again later

I want to send a fax
quiero mandar un fax
kyer-o man-**dar** oon faks

what's your fax number?
¿cuál es su número de fax?
*kwal es soo **noo**-me-ro de faks*

please resend your fax
por favor vuélvame a mandar su fax
*por fa-**bor bwel**-ba-me a man-**dar** soo faks*

the fax is engaged
el fax está ocupado
*el faks es-**ta** o-koo-**pa**-do*

can I send a fax from here?
¿puedo mandar un fax desde aquí?
pwe**-do man-**dar** oon faks **des**-de a-**kee

did you get my fax?
¿le llegó mi fax?
*le lyeg-**o** mee faks*

I want to send an e-mail
quiero mandar un e-mail
***kyer**-o man-**dar** oon **ee** mel*

what's your e-mail address?
cuál es su dirección de correo electrónico?
*kwal es soo dee-rekth-**yon** de kor-**re**-o e-lek-**tron**-ee-ko*

my e-mail address is...
mi dirección de correo electrónico es...
*mee dee-rekth-**yon** de kor-**re**-o e-lek-**tron**-ee-ko es...*

did you get my e-mail?
¿le llegó mi e-mail?
*le lyeg-**o** mee **ee**-mel*

do you have a fax?
¿tiene fax?
***tyen**-e faks*

I can't read it
no se entiende
*no se en-**tyen**-de*

NUMBERS

0	**cero** *ther-o*		
1	**uno** *oo-no*	1st	**primero** *pree-me-ro*
2	**dos** *dos*	2nd	**segundo** *se-goon-do*
3	**tres** *tres*		
4	**cuatro** *kwat-ro*	3rd	**tercero** *ter-ther-o*
5	**cinco** *theen-ko*		
6	**seis** *seyss*	4th	**cuarto** *kwar-to*
7	**siete** *syet-e*		
8	**ocho** *o-cho*	5th	**quinto** *keen-to*
9	**nueve** *nwe-be*		
10	**diez** *dyeth*	6th	**sexto** *seks-to*
11	**once** *on-the*		
12	**doce** *doth-e*	7th	**séptimo** *sep-tee-mo*
13	**trece** *treth-e*		
14	**catorce** *ka-torth-e*	8th	**octavo** *ok-ta-bo*
15	**quince** *keenth-e*		
16	**dieciséis** *dyeth-ee-seyss*	9th	**noveno** *no-be-no*
17	**diecisiete** *dyeth-ee-syet-e*		
18	**dieciocho** *dyeth-ee-o-cho*	10th	**décimo** *deth-ee-mo*
19	**diecinueve** *dyeth-ee-nwe-be*		

20	**veinte** *beyn-te*
21	**veintiuno** *beyn-te-oo-no*
22	**veintidós** *beyn-te-dos*
30	**treinta** *treyn-ta*
40	**cuarenta** *kwa-ren-ta*
50	**cincuenta** *theen-kwen-ta*
60	**sesenta** *se-sen-ta*
70	**setenta** *se-ten-ta*
80	**ochenta** *o-chen-ta*
90	**noventa** *no-ben-ta*
100	**cien** *thyen*
110	**ciento diez** *thyen-to dyeth*
200	**doscientos** *dos-thyen-tos*
500	**quinientos** *keen-yen-tos*
1000	**mil** *meel*
million	**un millón** *oon meel-yon*

ENERO	JANUARY
FEBRERO	FEBRUARY
MARZO	MARCH
ABRIL	APRIL
MAYO	MAY
JUNIO	JUNE
JULIO	JULY
AGOSTO	AUGUST
SEPTIEMBRE	SEPTEMBER
OCTUBRE	OCTOBER
NOVIEMBRE	NOVEMBER
DICIEMBRE	DECEMBER

LUNES	MONDAY
MARTES	TUESDAY
MIÉRCOLES	WEDNESDAY
JUEVES	THURSDAY
VIERNES	FRIDAY
SÁBADO	SATURDAY
DOMINGO	SUNDAY

what's the date?
¿qué fecha es hoy?
*kc **fe**cha es oy*

which day?
¿qué día?
*ke **dee**-ya*

which month?
¿qué mes?
ke mes

March 5th
el cinco de marzo
*el **theen**-ko de **mar**-tho*

July 6th
el seis de julio
*el seyss de **khoo**-lyo*

on Saturday
el sábado
*el **sa**-ba-do*

on Saturdays
los sábados
*los **sa**-ba-dos*

every Saturday
todos los sábados
***to**-dos los **sa**-ba-dos*

this Saturday
este sábado
***es**-te **sa**-ba-do*

next Saturdays
el próximo sábado
*el **prok**-see-mo **sa**-ba-do*

last Saturday
el sábado pasado
*el **sa**-ba-do pa-**sa**-do*

next week
la próxima semana
*la **prok**-see-ma se-**ma**-na*

last month
el mes pasado
*el mes pa-**sa**-do*

please can you confirm the date?
¿me puede confirmar la fecha?
*me **pwe**-de kon-feer-**mar** la **fe**-cha*

TIME

Note that throughout Europe the 24-hour clock is used much more widely than in the UK.

what time is it, please?
¿qué hora es, por favor?
*ke **o**-ra es por fa-**bor***

am
de la mañana
*de la man-**ya**-na*

pm
de la tarde
*de la **tar**-de*

it's 1 o'clock
es la una
*es la **oo**-na*

it's 2/3 o'clock
son las dos/tres
son las dos/tres

it's half past 8
son las ocho y media
*son las **o**-cho ee **med**-ya*

it is half past 10
son las diez y media
*son las dyeth ee **med**-ya*

in an hour
dentro de una hora
***den**-tro de **oo**-na **o**-ra*

in half an hour
dentro de media hora
***den**-tro de **med**-ya **o**-ra*

a quarter of an hour
un cuarto de hora
*oon **kwar**-to de **o**-ra*

three quarters of an hour
tres cuartos de hora
*tres **kwar**-tos de **o**-ra*

until 8 o'clock
hasta las ocho
***as**-ta las **o**-cho*

until 4 o'clock
hasta las cuatro
***as**-ta las **kwat**-ro*

at 10 am
a las diez de la mañana
*a las dyeth de la man-**ya**-na*

at 2200
a las veintidós horas
*a las beyn-tee-**dos** **o**-ras*

at midday
a las doce de la mañana
*a las **doth**-e de la man-**ya**-na*

at midnight
a medianoche
*a med-ya-**no**-che*

soon
pronto
***pron**-to*

later
más tarde
*mas **tar**-de*

ORDERING DRINKS

a black coffee
un café solo
*oon ka-**fe** so-lo*

a white coffee
un café con leche
*oon ka-**fe** kon **le**-che*

a tea
un té
oon te

with milk
con leche
*kon **le**-che*

with lemon
con limón
*kon lee-**mon***

a lager
una cerveza
***oo**-na ther-**be**-tha*

a dry sherry
un fino
*oon **fee**-no*

a hot chocolate with churros, please
un chocolate con churros, por favor
*oon cho-ko-**la**-te kon **choor**-ros por fa-**bor***

a bottle of mineral water
una botella de agua mineral
oo**-na bo-**tel**-ya de ag-wa mee-ne-**ral

sparkling
con gas
kon gas

still
sin gas
sin gas

the wine list, please
la carta de vinos, por favor
*la **kar**-ta de **bee**-nos por fa-**bor***

a glass of red wine
un vaso de tinto
*oon **ba**-so de **teen**-to*

a glass of white wine
un vaso de vino blanco
*oon **ba**-so de **vee**-no **blan**-ko*

a bottle of wine
una botella de vino
***oo**-na bo-**tel**-ya de **bee**-no*

red
tinto
***teen**-to*

white
blanco
***blan**-ko*

another bottle, please
otra botella, por favor
*o-tra bo-**tel**-ya por fa-**bor***

would you like a drink?
¿quiere tomar algo?
***kyer**-e to-**mar al**-go*

what will you have?
¿qué quiere tomar?
*ke **kyer**-e to-**mar***

ORDERING FOOD

*In Spain everything happens very late – including eating. Lunch is usually between 1 and 3pm and dinner between 8.30 and 11pm. Eating **tapas** in various bars is a good way of trying out different foods and allows you to eat earlier.*

can you recommend a good restaurant?
¿puede recomendarme un buen restaurante?
*pwe-de re-ko-men-**dar**-me oon bwen res-to-**ran**-te*

I'd like to book a table
quería reservar una mesa
*ke-**ree**-ya re-ser-**bar** oo-na **me**-sa*

for ... people
para ... personas
*pa-ra ... per-**so**-nas*

for tonight
para esta noche
*pa-ra es-ta **no**-che*

at 8 pm
a las ocho
*a las **o**-cho*

the menu, please
la carta, por favor
*la **kar**-ta por fa-**bor***

is there a dish of the day?
¿hay plato del día?
*aee **pla**-to del **dee**-ya*

have you a set-price menu?
¿tiene un menú del día?
***tyen**-e oon me-**noo** del **dee**-ya*

I'll have this
yo voy a tomar esto
*yo boy a to-**mar es**-to*

what do you recommend?
¿qué recomienda?
*ke re-kom-**yen**-da*

I don't eat meat
no como carne
*no **ko**-mo **kar**-ne*

do you have any vegetarian dishes?
¿tiene algún plato vegetariano?
***tyen**-e al-**goon pla**-to be-khe-tar-**ya**-no*

excuse me!
¡oiga, por favor!
*oy-ga por fa-**bor***

more bread
más pan
mas pan

more water
más agua
*mas **ag**-wa*

the bill, please
la cuenta, por favor
*la **kwen**-ta por fa-**bor***

SPANISH FOOD

THE CHARACTERISTICS OF THE REGIONS

One of the greatest pleasures of travelling in Spain is the discovery of regional cooking. Spain is a large country and its many provinces, so different in character and history, have developed their own distinctive dishes using the best of local produce.

Sampling the many tastes and textures of Spanish food couldn't be easier: just stop at a bar (**bar**) and order **tapas**. **Tapas** seem to have originated in Andalusia, but they are a way of life in the whole of Spain and have become fashionable even outside the country. They have the advantage of allowing you to taste lots of dishes at once, because, even though they can just be appetizers such as cured ham (**jamón serrano**) or cheese, they are often small portions of main dishes. In fact almost any dish can be served as a **tapa**: for instance, meat balls in sauce (**albóndigas**), squid rings fried in batter (**calamares fritos**), tripe (**callos**) and many more. Often each person orders two or three different **tapas**, so if you are eating with a group of friends you will have a dozen or so mini dishes to share. **Tapas** are ideal as a quick snack or light meal – often very welcome when you consider how late the meals are served in Spain. Some people have become addicted to visiting various bars, one after the other, to eat a few of their mini dishes instead of having a main meal. This can be great fun, especially in big cities, where there is an incredible variety of **tapas**. Be warned, however, that bars are generally quite cramped and don't have tables, so you have to eat and drink standing up, amid the hubbub of lively conversation.

The rich diversity of regional cooking, based on fresh local ingredients, reflects the diversity of Spain's landscape and climate. However, some elements are common to all areas, such as the use of **chorizo** (spicy pork sausage with paprika), peppers, olive oil and garlic. A number of regional dishes have become associated with Spain as a whole, such as **paella** (a rice dish), **tortilla** (potato omelette) and **fabada** (bean stew), but, fortunately, regional traditions continue to thrive.

SPANISH FOOD

NORTHERN SPAIN

The northern provinces of Galicia, Asturias, Cantabria and the Basque Country can be seen almost as one area, given their continuous coastline and rainy climate. But they do present vast differences gastronomically.

GALICIA (Santiago de Compostela)

The Galician coast is ideally suited to shellfish and other seafood. Octopus is prepared with paprika and olive oil. **Vieiras** (scallops) straight from the sea are flambéed and served in their shells, which symbolise the pilgrimages to Santiago de Compostela. But Galician meat is also excellent, especially the chickens from Villalba. The Galicians also use lots of greens, and their **caldo gallego** (Galician broth) is a marvellous chowder made with meats, beans and greens. **Empanada** is a local pie, filled with either meat or fish and flavoured with onion. Sweets include **episcopal** cakes (with fruit), **rosquillas** (biscuits) and almond cakes. Galician cheeses are the delicious **tetilla**, breast-shaped, and **perilla**, a smoked cheese.

ASTURIAS (Oviedo) and CANTABRIA (Santander)

Asturias and Cantabria grow many varieties of apple and produce wonderful **sidra** (cider), often used in dishes. Lush pastures ensure good milk, butter and cheeses, like the strong **cabrales-picón**, made with sheep, goat and cow's milk. The famous **fabada asturiana** (large butter beans), various cuts of pork and **morcilla**, a black pudding, is a winter warmer of the best kind. Lentils are the main ingredient of **cocido de lentejas**, a hotpot with **chorizo** (spicy red sausage) and seasonings. The area is rich in game. Among the fish dishes try Asturian **caldereta** (fish stew). To end a meal, rice pudding is a must, or the delicious **tocinillo del cielo**, made with egg yolks and caramelized sugar.

In the region of Cantabria, **ciervo** (venison) is very popular, as are **ternera** (veal) and **callos** (tripe). Chicken (**pollo**) served with rice is another speciality. Santander, a popular holiday resort, offers a special sardine stew, **sardinas a la santanderina**. **Arroz santanderino**, a dish eaten in the same town, consists of salmon and rice cooked in milk. Tuna, sea bream, hake and other fish also appear on the menu, prepared from local recipes. Desserts include egg custard and the **quesada**, a fresh cheese pudding rather like cheese cake. The best regional cheeses are those from Aliva and Tresviso.

SPANISH FOOD

THE BASQUE COUNTRY (San Sebastián), LA RIOJA (La Rioja) and NAVARRA (Pamplona)

The Basque Country is tucked away in the North, separated from France by the Pyrenees. Gastronomy is a serious business for the Basques. Many are very good cooks. The Basque language lends great exoticism to the names of the dishes, for example, **kokotxas** (a delicate hake dish) or **zurrukutuna** (salt cod with green peppers). In fact, despite the immense variety and quality of the fish along the coast, and the many excellent dishes prepared with all manner of seafood, salt cod is also very much appreciated in the Basque Country. The famous **bacalao a la vizcaína** - Biscay salt cod with peppers - is a national dish. San Sebastian, an elegant and beautiful tourist resort, has some of the best restaurants and best **tapas** to be found in Spain. Giant spider crab is one of the Basque specialities, among many others made with shellfish. Wild mushrooms abound here, as well as in Cantabria. For dessert try the luscious walnut pudding called **intxaursalsa**, **panchineta** (almond and custard tart) or the very strong **idiazábal** sheep's milk.

La Rioja is of course home to splendid wines but grapes and wine are not confined to this area and spill over into neighbouring provinces. Rioja's food is robust and distinctive, with wonderful vegetables, including asparagus, and meat dishes, such as the **patatas con chorizo** (potatoes with pork sausage). To follow, try some of the almond desserts, or the excellent local fruit.

Navarra may be almost Basque Country, in many respects, but its cuisine is much nearer to that of Aragón. Lots of game, pork and peppers are a constant there, as well as asparagus, wild mushrooms and artichokes. Many vegetables are used in **menestra**, a vegetable stew, which may include meat. Trout is again in evidence, fresh from mountain rivers and often served with cured ham. A special spicy sausage of this area is **chistorra**. The best local cheese is **roncal**, a hard smoked cheese made from sheep's milk.

SPANISH FOOD

EASTERN SPAIN

Navarra, La Rioja and Aragón are interior provinces full of contrasts but somehow united in their culinary traditions. They grow excellent fruit and vegetables, and peppers stand out as a favourite ingredient for many dishes. Gourmets will love the exquisite preserved **pimientos de piquillo**, on the menu in many of the best restaurants.

ARAGÓN (Saragossa)

Aragón is large and fertile. Lamb is a favourite meat, but pork and chicken are used almost as much and the local game is delicious too. The mighty Ebro river means lush fields and freshwater fish, with trout a speciality. This rich land is full of flavours and excellent but simple dishes, often enhanced with **chilindrón**, a local sauce made with tomatoes and red peppers. Mushrooms, artichokes, aubergines and asparagus are used frequently, spiced with the local **morcilla** (black pudding). **Migas** (fried breadcrumbs) are served in tasty dishes with ham, bacon and **chorizo**, but they also appear in an original dessert with grapes and chocolate. Chocolate is also a key ingredient in a rich gravy served as an accompaniment to partridge (**perdiz con chocolate)** Another local speciality is a pasty with sardines and peppers. Chocolate appears again with fruit for dessert, as well as **turrón** and pears in wine.

VALENCIA and MURCIA

The Levante is formed by Valencia and Murcia, provinces where rice is grown as a staple food. Rich fields yield a huge variety of fruit and vegetables. Oranges and early produce from enormous hothouses are exported all over Spain and abroad. **Ternera con naranja** (veal with orange) is a speciality and the long coastline provides excellent seafood, like sea bream (**dorada**) and king prawns. The main culinary experience of the Levante, however, is the **paella**, now a national dish. The real **paella valenciana** includes different kinds of seafood and chicken, or even pork, seasoned with saffron. But there are many other local rice dishes or **paellas** which are equally good. Game is also popular here, and the region is known for its fat snails and frogs. Almonds, locally grown dates and oranges are present in sugary desserts. **Turrón** (nougat made with almond and honey or sugar) is the main sweet in the area, the most

SPANISH FOOD

famous being the hard variety from Alicante and Valencia, although the soft **turrones**, which include eggs, are even nicer. Other memorable sweets are orange custard and **cabello de ángel** – literally angel's hair, which is a jam made from the stringy pulp of squash.

CATALONIA (Barcelona)

Catalonia is one of the most distinctive gastronomic regions in Spain, with the richest variety of dishes, prepared with great creativity and pride. The market in Barcelona must be one of the best in the world. The food is so beautifully displayed it's a pleasure just to look at it – but who could resist tasting in this city which boasts thousands of restaurants? Catalonia stretches from the Pyrenees to the Costa Dorada, a varied landscape producing abundant game, wild mushrooms, olive oil, cereals, grapes, beef, pork, lamb, goat's meat and milk, and of course seafood. **Zarzuela** is the local rich fish stew, but baby octopus and **parrilladas** (barbecued seafood) are also outstanding. The basis of most dishes is either **sofrito** (slowly fried onions in oil, with tomato and garlic), **picada** (a seasoning made with chopped parsley, almonds, pine nuts and garlic), **alioli** (a sauce of olive oil and garlic, for meat or fish) or the typically Catalan **samfaina** (pepper, aubergine and tomato, briefly cooked). While these recipes are preserved Catalonia will never lose its unique and marvellous flavours. Famous dishes include **escudela** (the local stew, with chickpeas, vegetables and meats), **calcotada** (roasted spring onion, laced with olive oil and almonds), **arroz a banda** (rice cooked with a variety of seafood and served with **alioli** or **romesco**, a local pepper sauce) and **cassolada** (pork and vegetable stew). **Butifarra** is the famous sausage, which can be white or black and goes into many dishes, like **habas a la catalana** (broad beans cooked in pork fat). For pudding, the choice is a rich caramel custard, **requesón** (soft whey cheese served with honey) or **garrotxa** (goat's cheese).

CENTRAL SPAIN

The immense plains of Central Spain (Extremadura, La Mancha and Northern Castile) are wheat and sheep land primarily. Bread and salads accompany the splendid roast lamb and other kinds of roast meat which

SPANISH FOOD

are characteristic of this area. In the restaurants of Madrid, however, you can find dishes from all the different regions of Spain as well as international cuisine. But **callos a la madrileña** (tripe Madrid style) and **cocido madrileño** (a substantial stew of meats, chickpeas and vegetables) are very much the capital's own versions of dishes that appear elsewhere in Spain.

MADRID

Although they live hundreds of miles from the sea, the people of Madrid have a gargantuan appetite for fish. All kinds of fish and shellfish are available, with the usual **angulas** (baby eels), **calamares** (squid) and **merluza** (hake) so prized by the Spaniards, as well as more expensive delicacies such as lobster, prawns and countless others. All over Madrid that most typical of Spanish breakfasts is served throughout the morning: **chocolate con churros** (sticks of fried batter dipped in hot chocolate).

CASTILE and LEÓN (Salamanca)

Old Castile and Léon are provinces of great historical interest and tradition but the severity of most of the landscape is reflected in the cooking, in which roasted meats predominate. Suckling pig and young lamb are outstanding. Some dishes are seasoned with cumin (a Moorish legacy) as well as cinnamon, aniseed and paprika. Game dishes are also common here, mainly partridge and quail. There are also a number of salt cod dishes. Other specialities are prepared with aubergines, green beans and potatoes. **Olla podrida** (a kind of slowly cooked ham and chickpea stew) is the local version of the **cocido**. This is also the region of splendid bread, which is used in various recipes, such as **sopa de ajo** (garlic soup) made with ham, seasonings and poached eggs. The region has marvellous cheeses, some cured and some fresh, including those from Burgos and Valladolid. The best sweets are the **yemas**, small yolk-shaped cakes made with lots of egg yolk and sugar, honeyed figs and **suspiros de monja** (literally nun's sighs, meringues served with thick custard).

CASTILE-LA MANCHA (Toledo)

A popular dish in Castile is **chanfaina** (a stew made of pig's liver, lungs and head) and although Spain is not known for a great variety of cakes,

SPANISH FOOD

there are some delicious sweet desserts worth noting, like **torrijas** (slices of bread dipped into wine and egg, and fried), **leche frita** (literally fried milk, consisting of a thick egg custard cut into pieces which are fried in breadcrumbs and served with sugar and cinnamon), and **roscos** (a kind of doughnut). Toledo, the old Spanish capital, is known for its **turrón** (nougat), the local version of a widespread Spanish speciality, made of honey and almonds.

La Mancha has to its credit the famous **manchego** cheese (made from sheep's milk), appreciated all over Spain. The whole of the Central region is rich in small game and although its austere culinary traditions reflect the harshness of the land and the extremes of cold and heat, it offers many imaginative dishes such as rabbit casserole, liver fried with oregano and **cordero asado a la manchega**, young lamb roasted on the spit.

EXTREMADURA (Cáceres)

The Extremadura region is grazing land where the most typical dishes have been created by those who tend the animals in the fields. Pork products are used a lot and the best ham in Spain comes from here. Bread is good and appears in various guises, such as **migas** (fried bread-crumbs, with strong seasonings and cured meats). Freshwater fish is used in **ajo de peces de río** (river fish with garlic) and there are also a few good salt cod dishes, like the **bacalao de convento**, made with spinach and potato. Another speciality is frogs' legs. Sweets consist mainly of small cakes, such as **rocas de candelilla** or **huevillos**, but the best dessert is a choice of excellent local fruit.

SOUTHERN SPAIN
ANDALUSIA (Seville)

All over Spain fried foods are a life-long passion, and nowhere is this passion stronger than in Andalusia. **Tortilla** (thick omelette made with potato and onion, but appearing in many other variations) is very much at home here, although **tortillas** are part of the Spanish repertoire all over the country. This region is vibrant, like its people. Lamb stews alternate with refreshing **gazpachos** (cold soups made with bread, tomatoes and various other ingredients, according to the locality) and garlic is con-

sumed in great quantities. Andalusia is also sherry country and this forti-
fied wine finds its way into many recipes with meat and fish (namely
monk fish), being especially good for enriching sauces, like in **riñones al
Jerez** (kidneys in sherry) Two of the great Andalucian specialities are
pato a la sevillana (duck cooked with wine and oranges, Seville fashion)
and **olla gitana** (gipsy soup) made with chickpeas, pork and vegetables
and flavoured with almonds and saffron. Andalusia is the essence of
Spain but the land is often poor, growing mainly olive trees and grapes.
However, good pork products, especially ham, are abundant. **Pescaito
frito** (small fried fish) is a popular dish around the coast, as well as
boquerones, fresh anchovies. The abundant olive oil is used in cooking
and salads, such as the **pipirrana** - a concoction of peppers, tomatoes,
fish and onion. This is the land of **tapas**, but sweets are also prominent
– an Arab legacy. For breakfast, **tortas** (cakes made with oil) are a must,
followed during the day by **yemas** (with egg yolks) and **cortadillos**, filled
with pumpkin jam, or **mostachones**, biscuits eaten with hot chocolate.

SPAIN'S ISLANDS

BALEARIC ISLANDS (Mallorca)

Within the Catalan region, the Balearic Islands have their own special
character. They are famous for their soups, either clear and light (meat or
fish broth) or thick and almost solid vegetable ones. Aubergines are used
a lot, mainly in **tumbet**, a layered vegetable dish, baked and served with
peppers and tomato sauce. Another sauce worth mentioning is of course
mayonnaise, which had its origin in Menorca. Eggs are used in various
specialities, such as **huevos estilo Soller**, prepared with the local
sausage (**sobrasada**) and a sauce. Chicken and turkey appear in lovely
dishes, but seafood really forms the best part of the Balearic repertoire,
for example, **caldereta de langosta** (lobster stew). **Coques** are served in
all the islands and are a kind of pizza with meat, fish or vegetables.
Visitors should try **ensaimada** a local spiral-shaped yeast bun, and
mahon, the splendid cow's cheese from Menorca.

SPANISH FOOD

CANARY ISLANDS (Tenerife)

The popular Canary Islands are a world apart, although food shows some influence from mainland Spain. One of the traditional staples is **gofio**, which can replace bread and is made with cornflour and shaped into a ball. Another local speciality is **mojo**, a sauce similar to South American **salsa**, which has many variations according to its use. A **mojo** can be made with peppers, spices and fresh coriander or it can be simply a basic oil, garlic and vinegar dressing, depending on what it is to be served with. **Puchero canario** is made with salted fish and potatoes and invariably served with one of those many sauces. Coriander leaves and watercress are two items that do not normally appear on Spanish tables but are popular here. Although the gastronomic repertoire of the Canary Islands is not vast, the distinctive local dishes are thoroughly enjoyable. Try the different kinds of soup, the simple and tasty meat or fish dishes spiced with cumin, herbs and red peppers, or **papas arrugadas** (literally wrinkled potatoes), new potatoes boiled in sea water then baked and served with fish. Curiously, a local black pudding is one of the ingredients of a dessert with raisins and slices of cake. Actually sweets are good and varied, using tropical fruit and honey. There is also an original goat's cheese, **majorero**, from the Fuerteventura island.

FESTIVE FOOD

Street and country festivals are very popular in Spain. Most of them are associated with religious celebrations, and normally dedicated to the patron saint of the local town or region. On such days people eat **buñuelos** (cakes or buns) and special festive meals are usually based on roasted meats, carefully prepared. In Galicia, saints' festivities are greeted with octopus spiced with paprika. In the Balearic Islands, **ensaimadas** filled with cream or custard are served at every celebration and even on Sundays. In Catalonia any feast is a good excuse for many cakes and sweets, like the **panelleta** (with pine nuts and almonds), while in the Alicante area, the **cocido de pelotas** is the preferred dish, a very rich, spicy stew with chickpeas and cabbage leaves stuffed with meat. In Murcia a memorable venison pie, the **pastel de cierva**, is chosen for these occasions. In Extremadura, the main festive dishes are **calanetas** and **frito**, made with kid and lamb.

Lent, and especially Good Friday, are salt cod days. These days are observed with simple food, and in the Levante there are dishes specially created with Lent in mind, made with potatoes, chickpeas or beans and greens (cauliflower, spinach). In the Balearic Islands you may find **ensaimadas** (yeast buns) with **sobrasada** (sausage).

For Easter, succulent roasted kid and lamb appear on the table, or even suckling pig. In Mallorca, excellent lamb pasties (**panades**) are served on this day, which also marks the start of the strawberry season all over the country. Almonds are also symbolic of Easter and are served roasted. Special cakes include **monas** (buns), **suspiros** (meringues) and many other sweets, like those splendid preserved chestnuts (**marrons glacés**).

Christmas is the time for **turrón**, that very special Spanish sweet which varies from region to region. The most famous **turrones** come from Valencia and Alicante (the hard versions); the others being made with ground almonds and eggs, are soft like almond paste. The best kind is from Jijona. In Toledo almonds are ground and the paste made into little figures, called **mazapán**, for which the city is known. **Roscón de reyes** (a round yeast cake with candied fruit) is also popular. **Polvorones** (crumbly cakes) originally from Andalusia are served everywhere. They are filled with almonds. There they also eat **amargos** (bitter almond sweets) and **tortada de almendra**, a delicious almond tart.

Turkey stuffed with pine nuts, raisins, and sausage meat is one of the traditional meals for Christmas, the best being arguably that from Gerona in Catalonia. Madrid, being so fond of fish, serves bream on this occasion, baked with lemon slices. In Majorca, **coques de torró** are sold at Christmas.

Almost every town and village has its own patron saint. The famous are:

San José (19th March), when the festival of the **Fallas** fills Valencia with processions of immense symbolic figures, afterwards burnt in huge bonfires. **Paellas** of all kinds are of course obligatory.

San Jorge (23rd April) is celebrated in the East with a special **paella** made with rice and two kinds of beans (black and white) called **Moros y Cristianos** (Moors and Christians) to commemorate Spain's victory over the invaders.

SPANISH FOOD

San Isidro (15th May) is Madrid's patron saint and the festivities go on for two weeks, when **buñuelos**, buns filled with cream, and **torrijas**, slices of bread dipped in egg and fried, served with sugar and cinnamon, are enjoyed by everyone, especially the children.

In Toledo, Corpus Christi is celebrated with a procession and the famous **mazapán**.

Catalonians greet San Juan's day (24th June) with bonfires and special cakes called **coques de la noche de San Juan**.

The festival of San Fermín (6th-14th July) brings all the **aficionados** (bull-fight lovers) to Pamplona in Navarra, for this is the time when bulls are let loose in the streets, to be challenged by all men who dare.

Santiago's Day (25th July) is celebrated in Galicia with **tarta de Santiago**, a flat almond cake which is traditionally decorated with a stencil of the sword of St James.

Asunción (15th August) means processions and festivals in many small towns.

San Mateo (19th September) is honoured mainly around Oviedo. This is also the grape harvest festival, when the traditional food is lamb, accompanied of course with generous quantities of wine.

On 12th October, Zaragoza celebrates the Virgen del Pilar, which is also Columbus Day. October is also the time of the saffron harvest in New Castile, where a 'saffron queen' is chosen.

All Saint's Day (**día de todos los santos**) is 1st November. **Buñuelos** (buns) are as usual sold at bakeries, as well as **huesos de santo** ('saint's bones', made from marzipan).

EATING OUT

As far as eating out in Spain is concerned, the general rule is that you must expect meals to be served late. It may be possible to start lunch at 1 pm but late lunches, starting at 2 pm at the earliest and going on until nearly 4 pm are more common. This also makes for a very late dinner, lighter in content than lunch. Dinner may start at 8.30 but more often than not at 9 or 10 pm. Breakfast is a light meal, usually consisting of white coffee and bread and butter or equivalent, but sometimes

SPANISH FOOD

Spaniards and travellers like to follow the old custom of a hot chocolate (thickened with flour) with **churros** (fried sticks of batter) to dip in it. This is served in some cafés and bars: look out for the notice. **Chocolate con churros** can be a fun and comforting breakfast to have, especially in winter. It is also a popular snack in the late afternoon (**merienda**).

Given the long gaps between meals, a snack is almost essential. In the evening this takes the form of **tapas**, which are served from 7 pm onwards at bars and **tascas** and very often consist simply of cured ham (**jamón serrano**) of quite good quality. More elaborate **tapas** may have to be searched for at specialist bars. This is a worthwhile effort, as already explained on page 62.

Please note that sometimes very simple **tapas**, like olives, can be free with your drink (generally serving beer or wine) but everything else is paid for separately, in most places. In most places snack bars and **tascas** display what they have on offer, which makes it easy to choose. You may want a **bocadillo** (sandwich made with French bread).

Sometimes **pinchos** (small **tapas**) are available as well, and it might be a good idea to try out a dish this way before committing oneself to a full **tapa**. On the other hand, one portion (**una ración**) may be ordered, if several people want to eat a little from the same dish.

TAPAS

aceitunas olives
aceitunas rellenas stuffed olives
albóndigas meat balls in sauce
boquerones fresh anchovies, generally fried
calamares a la romana fried squid rings in batter
calamares fritos fried squid
callos tripe (stew)
champiñones mushrooms
chorizo spicy red salami-type sausage
gambas prawns
gambas al ajillo prawns with garlic (grilled)
jamón serrano cured ham
mejillones mussels

SPANISH FOOD

pinchos *small servings usually Spanish omelette/cheese/ham with a slice of bread underneath*
ración *one portion*
tortilla *pieces of potato omelette*

EATING PLACES AND TYPE OF FOOD SERVED

Eating out is immensely popular in Spain, and it may be advisable to book beforehand if you want to be sure of a table at a special restaurant.
Bars serve drinks, coffee, breakfasts Spanish style. They may also offer **tapas**, **pinchos** (snacks) and **bocadillos** (sandwiches).
Tascas serve soft and alcoholic drinks and **tapas**.
Cafeterías serve some dishes and what may be called **platos combinados,** good for a light meal, as well as toasted sandwiches and even **pasteles** (cakes).
Pastelería (patisserie) serves all kinds of cakes and may have a counter for drinks.
Salón de té (tea room) is a more select establishment, serving **té** (tea) and cakes.
Marisquería is a bar or restaurant specialising in shellfish.
Mesón is a traditional-style tavern.
Restaurante is the general term for a restaurant.
Paradores are upmarket state-run hotels which also serve meals featuring regional dishes.
Hosterías are inns which also serve meals.
Merenderos are generally open-air places serving light food.
Ventas are simple road-side places serving snacks and drinks.

At restaurants, be prepared to spend time at the table. You can order à la carte or opt for the set menu, in which case you will be served more quickly. But take into consideration the large portions generally served. In Spain salads and vegetable dishes are considered as separate items and normally brought to the table before the main dish. You may choose soup to start with, perhaps a light **caldo** (clear broth) or thick **potaje** (thick broth/stew) unless your main course is a bean stew, which is normally quite liquid, almost like a soup. Or choose a fish or meat dish. Bread is always provided. For **postre** (dessert), fruit is the best choice, except when there are good local specialities. **Cena** (dinner or supper, given the hour) is generally a lighter version of the lunch menu.

READING THE MENU

La carta will indicate the various types of dishes served, dividing them into categories, i.e. soups, starters, fish dishes, and so on, in more or less detail, according to the type of restaurant.

Entremeses *Starters (also **entrantes fríos** or **calientes** – starters, cold or hot)*
Sopas *Soups*
Plato del día *Dish of the day*
Primer plato *First course*
Ensalada *Salad*
Verduras *Vegetables*
Huevos *Egg dishes*
Revueltos *Scrambled eggs (generally with something, like mushrooms)*
Pastas *Pasta dishes*
Arroz *Rice dishes*
Parrilladas *Grilled food*
Pescados *Fish dishes*
Carnes *Meats*
Postres *Desserts*
Quesos *Cheeses*

Entremeses *(or **entrantes**) Starters*
These can be hot or cold (**calientes** or **fríos**). Some of the dishes above, served as **tapas**, may also be offered as starters. In some establishments **entrantes** or **entremeses** are called **entretenimientos**, that is to say, something to entertain the palate while you wait for the main dish. **Sopas** (soups) are also considered as starters. Rice dishes may come into this category as **entrantes calientes** (hot starters), despite the fact that they may be as large as a main course. **Paella**, for instance, is normally only prepared for a minimum of two people, as are many other rice dishes.

DRINKS

DRINKS

Spain is a country well known for its wines but the Spanish also drink a lot of beer (**cerveza**) and other drinks. Tea (**té**) is drunk less in Spain than in many other countries, but coffee (**café**) and herbal teas (**tisanas** or **infusiones**) are popular. Drinking chocolate (**chocolate caliente**) is a breakfast favourite. Cider (**sidra**) is widely used in Asturias and the Basque Country, both for drinking and cooking. In summer it is nice to have **horchata** (a whitish drink made with tiger nuts), served very cool and especially popular in Madrid and the east of Spain. **Granizados** are among the best summer drinks, with fresh orange or lemon juice and ice.

WINES, SPIRITS AND OTHER ALCOHOLIC DRINKS

Wines are plentiful and generally of good quality. Each region produces its own wines and spirits. It is an interesting challenge to discover regional varieties, but one can always order **vino corriente** (table wine) as a safe choice for a pleasant and economical wine to have with a meal. Table wines (**vinos de mesa**) can be **tintos** (red), **blancos** (white) and **rosados** or **claretes** (rosé). Among such wines, those from Rioja are the best. Very fruity and fragrant, they can sometimes be quite alcoholic. Much of the wine drunk in restaurants and at home is young, fruity and excellent value. This is wine hasn't been left to age in barrels and is known as **de cosecha**. Wines **de crianza** are meant to have been left to age in wood, although many wines are now aged in bottles, for two or more years. Good bottled wines are classified according to their **denominación de origen** or **DO** to certify their origin. Here is a brief outline of some regional wines.

Rioja is the generic name given to wines from La Rioja region, the most outstanding of the thirty or so Spanish wine regions, itself three regions in one: the Lower (**Baja**), with stronger and full-bodied wines; the Upper (**Alta**) with excellent aged wines, less alcoholic than those from the **Baja**; and finally the **Alavesa**, with young, uncomplicated wines. They age well, as a rule. Look for **vino de gran reserva** if you want something really special.

The **Levante** and south-east areas have a great variety of wines from various **denominaciones de origen**, covering Valencia, Alicante, Utiel-Requena, Yecla and Jumilla. Between them there are whites and reds of remarkable quality, with a high alcohol content. There are also rosés, especially around Yecla, which are again quite alcoholic but very nice.

From the various **denominaciones** in **Catalonia**, most of which produce very good reds and some outstanding whites, the most famous are Penedés and Priorato, specialising respectively in whites and heavy, beautiful reds. Catalonia is also home for **cavas**, champagne-type sparkling wines (**champán**), from Sant Sadurní d'Anoia.

Castile is home to strong reds, some of them very famous. From its Rueda and Ribera del Duero regions, those produced in Quintanilla de Onésimo and Quintanilla de Arriba are exceptionally good. Production is not high, which makes for more expensive wines, with reds and whites of between 11 and 14% alcohol content.

La Mancha is another great wine region, with Valdepeñas, La Mancha and Méntrida sub-regions, the best known of which is Valdepeñas, with whites and reds of good quality. The alcohol content is not too high.

Andalusia embraces the sherry producing regions of Manzanilla-Sanlúcar de Barrameda, Málaga, Huelva, Montilla-Moriles and Jerez. Sherries and sweet dessert wines from Málaga are drunk in great quantities in Spain, but they are also very famous internationally. According to ageing methods and blending, sherries are classified into **fino**, dry and perfumed; **oloroso**, darker and with a stronger finish; **amontillado**, which has a lovely amber colour; **palo cortado**, which is a little lighter than **oloroso**; **raya**, also similar to **oloroso** but less strong; and **pedro ximénez**, which is really sweet and full of fruit. The **montilla-moriles** is strong and very dry, like the **manzanilla**. Wines from Málaga, the famous moscatels (made with muscat grape raisins), are really sweet, dark and fragrant. There are various málagas, such as the **pedro ximénez**, the moscatel proper or the **lácrima christi**.

From the **Balearic Islands**, there is wine produced on a small scale in Majorca. But Menorca produces gin and Ibiza has its own liqueur, normally drunk as a long drink, with ice. The **Canary Islands** produce some reasonably good wine for local consumption, and very nice **ron** (rum).

There are also many spirits to choose from, such as **coñac** (brandy), and liqueurs, as well as long drinks made from a mixture of wine and fruit (i.e. **sangría**), or a strong liqueur (i.e. **anís**, made with aniseed) with water.

DRINKS

agua mineral *mineral water*
aguardiente *a kind of clear grape brandy*
amontillado *medium-dry to dry sherry, very prized*
anís (seco or **dulce)** *aniseed liqueur, dry or sweet, normally drunk as a long drink with water and ice*
blanco y negro *a milky coffee with ice*
café *coffee*
café con leche *milky coffee (hot)*
café cortado *coffee with only a little milk*
café descafeinado *decaffeinated instant coffee*
café helado *coffee with ice*
café solo *black coffee*
carajillo *black coffee with brandy which may be set alight depending on regional customs*
cavas *champagne-style sparkling wines*
cerveza *beer – there are various good Spanish lager brands, such as San Miguel*
chocolate *drinking chocolate (thickened)*
coñac *brandy; it can be on the dry side or sweet and fragrant, as the Spaniards prefer*
crema *generic name given to smooth liqueurs, i.e.* **crema de naranja** *(orange cream)*
cremat *coffee with brandy and rum, served in Catalonia*
cubalibre *coca-cola mixed with rum or gin*
fino *the finest sherry, light and dry, equally good when young or after being aged*
ginebra *gin*
gran reserva *classification given to aged wines of exceptional quality*
granizado *fruit drink with crushed ice*
horchata de chufas *cool drink made with tiger nuts*
infusión *herbal tea*
jerez *sherry*
leche *milk*
leche caliente *hot milk*
leche fría *cold milk*
leche merengada *cool milk with meringue*
licor *liqueur*
limonada *lemonade (normally canned and fizzy)*

DRINKS

manzanilla *camomile tea (not to be confused with manzanilla as a sherry)*
manzanilla *very dry special sherry*
moscatel *muscat grape wine, sweet and fragrant*
oloroso *sweet, darker sherry*
pedro ximénez *sweet, rich sherry-type dessert wine*
queimada *warm drink made with **aguardiente** (clear brandy) sweetened with sugar and flamed, a speciality from Galicia*
rancio *sweet wine*
refresco de fruta *fruit drink with ice*
reserva *wines of good quality that have been aged, but not as long as **gran reserva***
ron *rum*
sangría *wine mixed with fruit and ice, with added water*
sidra *cider*
sifón *soda water*
té *tea*
té con leche *tea with milk*
té con limón *tea with lemon*
té helado *iced tea*
tisana *herbal tea*
vermú *vermouth*
vino *wine*
vino blanco *white wine*
vino clarete *rosé wine*
vino de mesa *table wine*
vino rosado *rosé wine*
vino tinto *red wine*
zumo *juice*
zumo de fruta *fruit juice*
zumo de albaricoque *apricot juice*
zumo de lima *lime juice*
zumo de limón *lemon juice*
zumo de melocotón *peach juice*
zumo de naranja *orange juice*
zumo de piña *pineapple juice*
zumo de tomate *tomato juice*

MENU READER

...a la/al *in the style of*
...a la brasa/barbacoa *barbecued*
...a la parrilla *grilled*
...a la plancha *grilled*
...a la romana *fried in batter (generally squid –* **calamares***)*
...al ajillo *with garlic*
...al horno *baked (in the oven)*
...al vapor *steamed*
aceite de oliva *olive oil*
aceitunas *olives*
aceitunas rellenas *stuffed olives*
acelgas *Swiss chard*
adobe, en *marinated*
ahumado *smoked*
ajetes *garlic shoots*
ajo *garlic*
ajo blanco *garlic and almond soup served cold*
ajo de las manos *sliced, boiled potatoes mixed with a garlic, oil and*
  vinegar dressing, and flavoured with red chillies
albahaca *basil*
albaricoque *apricot*
albóndigas *meat balls in sauce*
alcachofas *globe artichokes*
alcachofas a la vinagreta *artichokes served with a strong vinaigrette*
alcachofas con jamón *sautéed artichoke hearts with ham*
alcachofas rellenas *stuffed artichokes*
alcaparras *capers*
aliño *dressing*
alioli/all-i-oli *garlic mayonnaise*
almejas *clams/mussels*
almejas a la marinera *steamed clams/mussels cooked with parsley,*
  wine and garlic
almendras *almonds*
alubias *beans*
ancas de rana *frogs' legs*
anchoa *anchovy*
anguila *eel*
angulas *baby eels*
angulas al ajillo *baby eels cooked with garlic*
angulas en cazuelita *garlic flavoured, fried baby eels seasoned with*
  hot pepper

MENU READER

apio *celery*
arenque *herring*
arroz *rice*
arroz a banda *a dish of rice and fish. The dish is served in two courses:*
first the rice cooked with saffron is served and then the fish that has
been cooked in it
arroz a la levantina *rice with shellfish, onions, artichokes, peas, tomatoes*
and saffron
arroz a la valenciana *Valencian version of paella, usually with eel added*
arroz a la zamorana *rice with pork, peppers and garlic*
arroz blanco *boiled rice*
arroz con leche *rice pudding flavoured with cinnamon*
arroz con pollo *rice with boiled chicken, garnished with peas and pimento*
arroz negro *black rice (with squid and its ink)*
asado *roasted*
atún *tuna (usually fresh)*
atún con salsa de tomate *tuna fish in tomato sauce*
avellana *hazelnut*
azafrán *saffron*
bacalao *dried salt cod*
bacalao a la vizcaína *fried salt cod with a tomato, pepper, onion and*
garlic purée
bacalao al ajo arriero *salt cod fried with garlic to which is added vinegar,*
paprika and chopped parsley
bacalao con patatas *salt cod slowly baked with potatoes, peppers,*
tomatoes, onions, olives and bay leaves
bacalao de convento *salt cod cooked with spinach and potato*
bacalao al pil-pil *a Basque speciality – salt cod cooked with garlic and*
olive oil
bandeja de quesos *tray of different kinds of cheeses*
berenjena *aubergine (eggplant)*
berenjenas a la catalana *aubergines with tomato sauce, Catalan style*
berenjenas rellenas *stuffed aubergines (usually with mince)*
berenjenas salteadas *aubergines sautéed with tomatoes and onions*
besugo *bream*
bistec *steak*
bizcocho *sponge finger*
bizcocho borracho *sponge soaked in wine and syrup*
bocadillo *sandwich (French bread)*
bogavante *lobster*

MENU READER

bonito *tunny fish, lighter than tuna, good grilled*
boquerones *fresh anchovies*
boquerones fritos *fried anchovies*
buñuelos *type of fritter. Savoury ones are filled with cheese, ham, mussels or prawns. Sweet ones can be filled with fruit*
buñuelos de bacalao *dried salt cod fritters*
butifarra *special sausage from Catalonia*
butifarra blanca *white sausage containing pork and tripe*
butifarra negra *black sausage containing pork blood, belly and spices*
caballa *mackerel*
cabello de ángel *jam made from squash*
cabrito *kid (goat)*
cabrito al horno *roast kid*
cacahuete *peanut*
cachelada *chopped boiled potatoes and cabbage with garlic, red pepper and fried bacon. Often served with* **chorizo**
calabacines *courgettes*
calabacines rellenos *stuffed courgettes*
calabaza guisada *stewed pumpkin*
calamares *squid*
calamares a la romana *fried squid rings in batter*
calamares en su tinta *squid cooked in its own ink*
calamares fritos *fried squid*
calamares rellenos *stuffed squid*
calcotada *roasted spring onion laced with olive oil and almonds*
caldeirada *fish soup from Galicia*
caldereta *stew/casserole*
caldereta de cordero *lamb casserole*
caldereta de langosta *lobster stew*
caldereta de pescado *fish stew*
caldo *clear soup, consommé*
caldo de pescado *fish soup*
caldo gallego *clear soup with green vegetables, beans and pork*
caliente *hot*
callos *tripe*
callos a la madrileña *fried tripe casseroled in a spicy paprika sauce with tomatoes and chorizo sausage*
camarones *shrimps*
canela *cinnamon*
cangrejo *crab*
caracoles *snails*

caracoles de mar *winkles*
caracolillos *winkles*
cardo *cardoon, plant related to the artichoke*
carne *meat*
carne picada *minced meat*
carnero *mutton*
cassolada *pork and vegetable stew*
castaña *chestnut*
cebolla *onion*
cebollas rellenas *stuffed onions*
centollo *spider crab*
cerdo *pork*
cerdo asado *roast pork*
cerezas *cherries*
champiñones *mushrooms*
chanfaina *a stew made from pig's liver and other parts such as lungs*
chanquetes *small fish rather like whitebait*
chilindrón *tomato and chilli sauce*
chistorra *spicy sausage from Navarra*
chorizo *spicy red sausage. The larger type is eaten like salami, the thinner type is cooked in various dishes*
choto *young kid*
choto albaicinero *kid fried with garlic*
chuleta *chop*
chuleta de cerdo *pork chop*
chuleta de ternera *veal chop*
chuletas de cordero *grilled lamb chops*
chuletón *large chop*
churrasco *barbecued meat*
churros *fried batter sticks sprinkled with sugar, usually eaten with thick hot chocolate*
ciervo *deer (venison)*
ciruelas *plums*
coca (coques) *type of pizza with meat, fish or vegetables served in the Balearic Islands. They can also be sweet*
cochinillo *roast suckling pig*
cocido *stew made with various meats, vegetables and chickpeas. There are regional variations of this dish and it is worth trying the local version*
cocido de lentejas *thick stew of lentils and chorizo sausage*
cocido de pelotas *a rich spicy stew with chickpeas and cabbage leaves stuffed with meat*

MENU READER

coco *coconut*
cóctel de gambas *prawn cocktail*
codillo de cerdo *pig's trotter*
codonices asadas *roast quail*
codoniz *quail*
col *cabbage*
coles de Bruselas *Brussels sprouts*
coliflor *cauliflower*
comino *cumin*
conejo *rabbit*
consomé al jerez *consommé with sherry*
consomé de gallina *chicken consommé*
copa *goblet*
copa de helado *assorted ice cream served in a goblet*
coques *see* **coca**
coques de torró *wafers filled with almonds, sold at Christmas in Mallorca*
cordero *lamb*
cordero al chilindrón *lamb in a spicy pepper sauce*
cordero asado *roast lamb*
cordero asado a la manchega *spit-roasted young lamb*
cordero relleno trufado *lamb stuffed with truffles*
costillas *ribs*
costillas de cerdo *pork ribs*
crema *cream soup*
crema catalana *similar to crème brûlée*
crema de espárragos *cream of asparagus*
crema de tomate *cream of tomato soup*
croquetas *croquettes*
croquetas de camarones *shrimp croquettes*
crudo *raw*
culantro *coriander*
dátiles *dates*
dorada *sea bream*
dorada a la sal *sea bream cooked in the oven, covered only with salt, forming a crust*
dorada al horno *baked sea bream*
embutido *sausage*
empanada *pie filled with meat or fish and vegetables*
empanadilla *pasty/small pie filled with meat or fish*
empanado *breadcrumbed and fried*
ensaimada *sweet spiral-shaped yeast bun from Mallorca*

ensalada (mixta/verde) *salad (mixed/green)*
ensalada de la casa *lettuce, tomato and onion salad (may include tuna)*
ensalada de huevos *salad with hard boiled eggs*
ensaladilla *diced cooked vegetables in mayonnaise*
entrecot *entrecôte steak*
entremeses *starters*
entremeses de fiambre *cold meat hors d'œuvres*
entremeses de pescado *fish hors d'œuvres*
escabeche, en *pickled*
escabeche de pescado *fish marinated in oil and served cold*
escalfado *poached*
escalivada *salad of chargrilled vegetables such as peppers and aubergines soaked in olive oil*
escalope de ternera *veal escalope*
escarola *endive*
escudella *meat, vegetable and chickpea soup. Catalan version of* **cocido**
escudilla de pages *white bean, sausage, ham and pork soup*
espárragos *asparagus*
espárragos con mahonesa *asparagus with mayonnaise*
espinacas gratinadas *spinach au gratin*
estofado *braised*
estofado de cordero *lamb stew*
estofado de ternera *veal stew*
estragón *tarragon*
fabada *pork, ham, black pudding, beans and sausage stew. It can vary from region to region*
fabada asturiana *large butter beans, pork and black pudding stew*
faisán *pheasant*
faves *large white haricot beans*
fiambre *cold meat*
fiambre de tenera *veal pâté*
fiambres surtidos *assorted cold meats*
fideos *noodles/thin ribbons of pasta*
fideuà amb marisc *seafood dish with fine pasta (vermicelli)*
filete *fillet steak*
filete de ternera *veal steak*
filete a la plancha *grilled fillet steak*
filetes de lenguado *sole fillets*
flan *type of crème caramel*
frambuesas *raspberries*
fresas *strawberries*

MENU READER

fresas con nata *strawberries and cream*
frijoles *beans (name used in the Canary Islands)*
frío *cold*
frito *fried*
fritura de pescado *fried assortment of fish*
fruta *fruit*
fruta del tiempo *fruit in season*
frutos secos *nuts (general term)*
galleta *biscuit*
gambas *prawns*
gambas a la plancha *grilled prawns*
gambas al ajillo *prawns with garlic (grilled)*
gambas pil-pil *sizzling prawns cooked with chillies*
ganso *goose*
garbanzos *chickpeas*
garbanzos con espinacas *chickpeas with spinach*
garrotxa *goat's cheese*
gazpacho *traditional cold soup of Spain. There are many different recipes. Basic ingredients are water, tomatoes, onion, cucumber, green pepper, fresh breadcrumbs, vinegar and olive oil. Should always be served chilled.*
gazpacho extremeño *a version of gazpacho made with finely chopped green peppers and onions*
gofio *toasted cornmeal often rolled into balls and eaten as a bread substitute in the Canary Islands*
gratinado *au gratin*
grelos *young turnip tops*
guindilla *chilli*
guisado *stew or casserole*
guisantes *peas*
guisantes a la española *boiled peas with ham, lettuce, carrots and onions*
habas *broad beans*
habas a la catalana *broad beans cooked in pork fat often served with sausage*
habas con jamón *broad beans with ham*
hamburguesa *hamburger*
helado *ice cream*
hervido *boiled*
hígado *liver*
hígado con cebolla *fried calf's liver with onions*
higos *figs*

MENU READER

higos secos *dried figs*
huevos *eggs*
huevos a la española *stuffed eggs with a cheese sauce*
huevos a la flamenca *baked eggs with tomatoes, peas, peppers, asparagus and sausage*
huevos al plato *eggs baked in butter*
huevos con jamón *fried eggs and ham*
idiazábal *smoked sheep's milk cheese from the Basque country*
intxaursalsa *whipped cream and walnut pudding*
jamón *ham*
jamón de jabugo *Andalucian ham*
jamón de York *cooked ham*
jamón serrano *aromatic, dark red cured ham*
jengibre *ginger*
jibia or **jivia** *cuttlefish*
judías *beans*
judías verdes *green beans*
judías verdes a la castellana/española *boiled green beans mixed with fried parsley, garlic and pimentos*
jurel *horse mackerel scad*
kokotxas *pieces of hake usually fried*
lacón con grelos *salted pork with young turnip tops and white cabbage*
langosta *lobster*
langosta a la catalana *potatoes with a lobster filling served with mayonnaise*
langostinos *king prawns/crayfish*
langostinos a la plancha *grilled king prawns*
langostinos a la vinagreta *casseroled crayfish with hardboiled eggs served in a vinaigrette sauce*
laurel *bay leaf*
lechazo *young lamb (roasted)*
leche *milk*
leche frita *very thick custard dipped into an egg and breadcrumb mixture, fried and served hot in squares*
leche merengada *milk and egg sorbet*
lechuga *lettuce*
legumbres *fresh or dried pulses*
lenguado *sole*
lenguado a la romana *sole fried in batter*
lenguados fritos *fried fillets of sole often served on a bed of mixed sautéed vegetables*

MENU READER

lenguados rellenos *fillets of sole stuffed with shrimps or prawn*
lentejas *lentils (very popular in Spain)*
liebre *hare*
liebre estofada *stewed hare*
limón *lemon*
lomo *loin of pork*
longaniza *spicy pork sausage*
longaniza con judías blancas *spicy pork sausage with white beans*
lubina *sea bass/turbot*
lubina a la asturiana *Asturian-style sea bass, with cider*
lubina al horno *baked turbot with potatoes, onion, tomato and garlic*
macarrones *macaroni*
macedonia de fruta *fruit salad*
mahonesa *mayonnaise*
maiz *sweetcorn*
majorero *goat's cheese from Canary Islands*
manos de cerdo *pig's trotters*
mantequilla *butter*
manzana *apple*
manzanas rellenas *stuffed baked apples*
mariscada *mixed shellfish*
marisco *shellfish*
mayonesa *mayonnaise*
mazapán *marzipan*
medallón *steak/slice/medallion*
mejillones *mussels*
mejillones a la marinera *mussels cooked in wine*
mejillones al vapor *mussels (steamed)*
melecotón *peach*
melón *melon*
melón con jamón *melon and cured ham*
menestra de verduras *fresh vegetable stew often cooked with ham*
merluza *hake, one of the most popular fish in Spain*
merluza a la asturiana *boiled hake served with mayonnaise and garnished with hard boiled eggs*
merluza con sidra *hake baked with clams, onions and cider*
merluza en salsa verde *hake with green sauce (with parsley)*
mermelada *jam*
mero *grouper*
miel *honey*
migas *breadcrumbs usually fried in garlic with diced ham*

migas con jamón *ham with breadcrumbs*
migas extremeñas *breadcrumbs fried with egg and spicy sausage*
mojama *cured tuna fish, a delicacy*
mojo *a sauce made from olive oil, vinegar, cumin and chilli. Predominantly found in the Canary Islands*
mojo verde *mojo made with fresh coriander*
mollejas *sweetbreads*
mollejas de ternera *calves' sweetbread*
morcilla *black pudding*
moros y cristianos *boiled rice, black beans and onions served with garlic sausage*
mostaza *mustard*
nabo *turnip*
naranja *orange*
nata *cream*
natillas *custard*
navajas *razor clams*
nectarinas *nectarines*
nuez *walnut*
nuez moscada *nutmeg*
olla gitana *thick stew/soup made with chickpeas, pork and vegetables and flavoured with almonds and saffron*
olla podrida *thick ham, vegetable and chickpea stew/soup*
oreja de cerdo a la plancha *grilled pigs's ears*
ostras *oysters*
paella *one of the most famous of Spanish dishes. Paella varies from region to region but usually consists of rice, chicken, shellfish, vegetables, garlic and saffron. The dish's name derives from the large shallow pan in which it is cooked*
paella de mariscos *a rice and shellfish paella*
pan *bread*
pan de higos *dried figs*
panades *lamb pasties eaten at Easter in Balearics*
panchineta *almond and custard tart*
panecillo *bread roll*
panelleta *small cakes with pine nuts and almonds*
papas arrugadas *potatoes cooked in their skins with garlic*
parrillada *mixed grill (can be meat or fish)*
parrillada de mariscos *mixed grilled shellfish*
pasas *raisins*
pasta *pasta*

MENU READER

pastel *cake/pastry*
pastel de carne *pie (meat)*
pastel de ternera *veal pie*
patatas *potatoes*
patatas arrugadas *potatoes cooked in their skins with garlic*
patatas bravas *sliced boiled potatoes mixed with a garlic, oil and vinegar dressing and flavoured with red chilli peppers*
patatas con chorizo *potatoes cooked with chorizo sausage*
patatas fritas *chips*
patatas nuevas *new potatoes*
pato *duck*
pato a la sevillana *joints of wild duck cooked with sherry, onion, tomatoes, herbs and garlic, served in an orange and olive sauce*
pavo *turkey*
pavo relleno *stuffed turkey*
pechuga de pollo *chicken breast*
pechugas en bechamel *chicken breast in bechamel sauce*
pepino *cucumber*
pepitoria de pavo/pollo *turkey/chicken casserole*
pera *pear*
percebes *goose-neck barnacle, a Galician shellfish*
perdices con chocolate *partridge with a chocolate sauce*
perdiz *partridge*
perejil *parsley*
pescado *fish*
pescaíto frito *mixed fried fish*
pez espada *swordfish, very good grilled or fried*
picada *seasoning of chopped parsley, almonds, pine nuts and garlic*
pimienta *pepper (spice)*
pimientos *red, green, yellow peppers, one of the typical Spanish flavours*
pimientos de piquillo *pickled red peppers*
pimientos rellenos *peppers stuffed with meat or fish*
piña *pineapple*
pinchos *small serving of usually Spanish omelette/cheese/ham with a slice of bread underneath*
pinchos morunos *meat grilled on a skewer*
piperrada *type of omelette with red peppers, green beans and ham*
pipirrana *a dish of fish, peppers, tomatoes, hardboiled eggs and onions*
pisto *a mixture of sautéed peppers, onions, aubergines, tomatoes, garlic and parsley. Similiar to French ratatouille. Served hot or cold*
plátano *banana*

platija *plaice (flounder)*
plato *dish*
platos combinados *quick meal usually eaten in a cafeteria; consists of assorted food served together on one plate*
plato del día *dish of the day*
pollo *chicken*
pollo al chilindrón *chicken cooked with onion, ham, garlic, red pepper and tomatoes*
pollo asado *roast chicken*
pollo con patatas *chicken and chips*
pollo en pepitoria *breaded chicken pieces fried, then casseroled with herbs, almonds, garlic and sherry*
pollo estofado *chicken stewed with potatoes, mushrooms, shallots, bay leaves and mushrooms*
pollo relleno *stuffed chicken*
polvorones *very crumbly cakes made with almonds and often eaten with a glass of **anís***
pomelo *grapefruit*
porras *fried sticks of batter*
postres *desserts*
potaje *thick soup/stew often with pork and pulses*
potaje murciano *red bean, french bean and rice soup*
pote *thick soup with beans and sausage having many regional variations*
pote gallego *thick soup made with cabbage, white kidney beans, potatoes, pork and sausage*
primer plato *first course*
puchero *hotpot made from meat or fish*
puchero canario *salted fish and potatoes served with **mojo** sauce*
pudín *crème caramel*
puerros *leeks*
pulpo *octopus*
puré de garbanzos *thick chickpea soup*
puré de patatas *mashed potatoes*
quesada *dessert similar to cheesecake*
queso *cheese*
queso de Burgos *curd cheese from Castile*
queso de cabrales *strong blue cheese from Asturias*
questo de Mahón *strong hard cheese from Menorca*
queso de Roncal *hard smoked sheep's cheese*
queso fresco *curd cheese*
queso manchego *hard sheep's curd cheese from La Mancha*

MENU READER

rábanos radishes
rabo de toro bull's tail, usually cooked in a stew
ración portion of tapas
rape monkfish
rape a la marinera monkfish cooked with wine
raya skate
rebozado in batter
relleno stuffed
remolacha beetroot
repollo cabbage
requesón cream cheese similar to cottage cheese
revuelto scrambled eggs often cooked with another ingredient
revuelto de champiñones scrambled eggs with mushrooms
revuelto de espárragos scrambled eggs with asparagus tips
revuelto de espinacas scrambled eggs with spinach
revuelto de gambas scrambled eggs with prawns
revuelto de morcilla scrambled eggs with blood pudding/sausage
riñones al jerez kidneys in sherry sauce
rodaballo turbot
romero rosemary
romesco sauce made of almonds and hazelnuts with mild chilli. Often
served with fish and chicken
rosco doughnut
roscón de reyes a large bun-like cake in the shape of a ring, similar to
Italian panettone and eaten at Epiphany
salchichas sausage
salchichón salami-type sausage
salmón salmon
salmón a la parilla grilled salmon
salmón a la ribereña salmon fried with ham, with cider sauce
salmón ahumado smoked salmon
salmonete red mullet
salmonete frito fried red mullet
salsa sauce
salsa de tomate tomato sauce
salsa romesco sauce made of almonds and hazelnuts with mild chilli.
Often served with fish and chicken
salsa verde garlic and parsley sauce
salteado sauteed
samfaina a dish of peppers, aubergines and tomatoes to which meat is
often added

sandía water melon
sandwich sandwich (usually toasted)
sardinas sardines
sardinas a la santanderina sardines cooked with tomato, Santander style
sardinas asadas barbecued sardines
sardinas frescas/fritas fresh/fried/sardines
sardinas rebozadas sardines cooked in batter
sargo type of bream
seco dry
sesos brains
sesos a la romana brains fried in batter
sesos fritos fried brains
setas wild mushrooms
sidra cider
sobrasada a fatty paprika-flavoured pork sausage from Mallorca
sofrito slowly fried onions with garlic and tomato
solomillo sirloin
solomillo de ternera veal sirloin
sopa soup
sopa castellana garlic and chickpea soup
sopa de ajo garlic soup with bread. May contain poached egg or ham
sopa de arroz rice soup
sopa de cebolla onion soup
sopa de fideos noodle soup
sopa de gallina chicken soup
sopa de rabo oxtail soup
sopa mallorquina tomato, onion and pepper soup thickened with
  breadcrumbs
sopa de mariscos shellfish soup
sopa de pescado fish soup
sopa de pollo chicken soup
sopa de verduras vegetable soup
sorbete sorbet
sorbetes de frutas fruit sorbets
suquet fish, potato and tomato stew
suspiros meringues
suspiros de monja meringues served with thick custard
tapas appetizers
tarta cake/tart/gâteau
tarta de manzana apple tart

SPANISH FOOD

tarta de Santiago *flat almond cake*
tarta helada *ice-cream cake*
ternera *veal*
ternera con naranja *veal cooked with orange*
ternera rellena *stuffed veal*
tetilla *soft white cheese made in the form of a woman's breast*
tocino *bacon*
tomates *tomatoes*
tomates rellenos *stuffed tomatoes*
tomillo *thyme*
torrija *bread dipped in milk and then fried and sprinkled with sugar
and cinnamon*
tortilla (española) *omelette cooked with potatoes. Often sliced and
served as a tapa*
tortilla con espárragos *asparagus omelette*
tortilla de champiñones *mushroom omelette*
tortilla de chorizo *omelette with chorizo sausage*
tortilla de jamón *ham omelette*
tortilla murciana *tomato and pepper omelette*
trucha *trout*
trucha a la navarra *trout stuffed with ham slices*
trucha con almendras *fried trout with almonds*
tumbet *layers of peppers, aubergine and tomato cooked with potato
in an earthenware dish*
turrón *nougat*
turrón de Alicante *hard nougat*
turrón de Jijona *soft nougat*
txangurro *spider crab*
uvas *grapes*
verduras *vegetables*
vieiras *scallops*
vieiras de Santiago *scallops served in their shell. Cooked in brandy,
topped with breadcrumbs and grilled*
vinagre *vinegar*
vinagreta *vinaigrette*
yemas *small cakes that look like egg yolks*
zanahorias *carrots*
zarzuela de mariscos *mixed seafood with wine and saffron from Catalonia*
zarzuela de pescado *fish stew*
zurrukutuna *salt cod cooked with green peppers*

DICTIONARY
english-spanish
spanish-english

A

a(n) un(a)
abbey la abadía
abortion el aborto
abortion pill la píldora abortiva
about (concerning) sobre
  about 2 o'clock alrededor de las dos
above arriba ; por encima
abroad en el extranjero
abscess el absceso
accelerator el acelerador
accent (pronunciation) el acento
to accept aceptar
accident el accidente
accommodation el alojamiento
to accompany acompañar
account (bank, etc) la cuenta
to ache doler
  my head aches me duele la cabeza
  my tooth aches me duele una muela
acid el ácido
actor/actress el actor/la actriz
adaptor (electrical) el adaptador
adder la víbora
address la dirección
  what is the address? ¿cuál es la dirección?
address book la libreta de direcciones
admission charge/fee el precio de entrada
adult el/la adulto(a)
  for adults para adultos
advance: *in advance* por adelantado
advertisement el anuncio
to advise aconsejar
aeroplane el avión
aerosol el aerosol
to be afraid of tener miedo de
after después

after lunch después de almorzar
afternoon la tarde
  this afternoon esta tarde
  in the afternoon por la tarde
  tomorrow afternoon mañana por la tarde
aftershave el aftershave
again otra vez
against contra
age la edad
agency la agencia
ago: *a week ago* hace una semana
to agree estar de acuerdo
agreement el acuerdo
AIDS el sida
airbag (in car) el airbag
air conditioning el aire acondicionado
  is there air conditioning? ¿Hay aire acondicionado?
air freshener el ambientador
airline la línea aérea
air mail: *by airmail* por avión
air mattress el colchón inflable
airplane el avión
airport el aeropuerto
airport bus el autobús del aeropuerto
air ticket el billete de avión
aisle el pasillo
alarm la alarma
alarm clock el despertador
alcohol el alcohol
alcohol-free sin alcohol
alcoholic alcohólico(a)
  is it alcoholic? ¿tiene alcohol?
all todo(a)/todos(as)
allergic to alérgico(a) a
  I'm allergic to soy alérgico(a) a
allergy la alergia
to allow permitir
  to be allowed estar permitido
all right (agreed) de acuerdo
  (OK) vale
  are you all right? ¿está bien?

almond la almendra
almost casi
alone solo(a)
alphabet el alfabeto
also también
altar el altar
always siempre
am *see* (to be) **GRAMMAR**
amber *(traffic light)* amarillo
ambulance la ambulancia
America América del Norte
American norteamericano(a)
amount: total amount el total
anaesthetic la anestesia
  local anaesthetic la anestesia
  local
  general anaesthetic la anestesia
  general
anchor el ancla
anchovy *(fresh)* el boquerón
  (salted) la anchoa
ancient antiguo(a)
and y
angel el ángel
angina la angina de pecho
angry enfadado(a)
animal el animal
aniseed el anís
ankle el tobillo
anniversary el aniversario
annual anual
another otro(a)
  another beer, please otra
  cerveza, por favor
answer la respuesta
to answer responder
answerphone el contestador
  automático
ant la hormiga
antacid el antiácido
antibiotic el antibiótico
antifreeze el anticongelante
antihistamine el antihistamínico
antique shop el anticuario
antiques las antigüedades

antiseptic el antiséptico
any alguno(a)
  have you any pears? ¿tiene
  peras?
apartment el apartamento
apéritif el aperitivo
appendicitis la apendicitis
apple la manzana
apple juice el zumo de manzana
application form el impreso de
  solicitud
appointment *(meeting)* la cita
  (dentist, hairdresser) la hora
apricot el albaricoque
April abril
apron el delantal
architect el/la arquitecto(a)
architecture la arquitectura
are *see* (to be) **GRAMMAR**
arm el brazo
armbands *(to swim)* los manguitos
  de nadar
armchair el sillón
aromatherapy la aromaterapia
to arrange organizar
to arrest detener
arrival la llegada
to arrive llegar
art el arte
art gallery el museo de arte
arthritis la artritis
artichoke la alcachofa
artist el/la artista
ashtray el cenicero
to ask *(question)* preguntar
  (to ask for something) pedir
asparagus los espárragos
aspirin la aspirina
  soluble aspirin la aspirina
  esfervescente
asthma el asma
  I have asthma tengo asma
at a ; en
  at home en casa
  at 8 o'clock a las ocho

97

a

at once ahora mismo
at night por la noche
Atlantic Ocean el Océano Atlántico
to attack atacar
attic el ático
attractive *(person)* guapo(a)
aubergine la berenjena
auction la subasta
audience el público
August agosto
aunt la tía
au pair el/la au pair
Australia Australia
Australian australiano(a)
author el/la autor(a)
automatic car el coche automático
auto-teller el cajero automático
autumn el otoño
available disponible
avalanche la avalancha
avenue la avenida
avocado el aguacate
to avoid *(obstacle)* evitar
  (person) esquivar
awful espantoso(a)
axle el eje

B

baby el bebé
baby food los potitos
baby milk la leche infantil
baby's bottle el biberón
babyseat *(in car)* el asiento del bebé
babysitter el/la canguro
baby wipes las toallitas infantiles
bachelor el soltero
back *(of body)* la espalda
backpack la mochila
bacon el beicon
bad *(weather, news)* mal/malo(a)
  (fruit and vegetables) podrido(a)
bag la bolsa

baggage el equipaje
baggage allowance el equipaje permitido
baggage reclaim la recogida de equipajes
bail bond la fianza
bait *(for fishing)* el cebo
baked al horno
baker's la panadería
balcony el balcón
bald *(person)* calvo(a)
  (tyre) gastado(a)
ball *(large: football, etc)* el balón
  (small: golf, tennis, etc) la pelota
ballet el ballet
balloon el globo
banana el plátano
band *(rock)* el grupo
bandage la venda
bank el banco
  (river) la ribera
bank account la cuenta bancaria
banknote el billete
bar el bar
barbecue la barbacoa
  to have a barbecue hacer una barbacoa
barber's la barbería
barcode el código de barras
to bark ladrar
barn el granero
barrel *(wine/beer)* el barril
basement el sótano
basil la albahaca
basket la cesta
basketball el baloncesto
bat *(baseball, cricket)* el bate
  (creature) el murciélago
bath el baño
  to have a bath bañarse
bathing cap el gorro de baño
bathroom el cuarto de baño
  with bathroom con baño
battery *(radio, camera, etc)* la pila
  (in car) la batería

bay (along coast) la bahía
Bay of Biscay el Mar Cantábrico
bay leaf la hoja de laurel
to be see (to be) GRAMMAR
beach la playa
  private beach la playa privada
  sandy beach la playa de arena
beach hut la caseta de playa
bean la alubia
  broad bean el haba
  french/green bean la judía verde
  soya bean la alubia de soja
  kidney bean la alubia pinta
bear (animal) el oso
beard la barba
beautiful hermoso(a)
beauty salon el instituto de belleza
because porque
bed la cama
  double bed la cama de matrimonio
  single bed la cama individual
  sofa bed el sofá-cama
  twin beds las camas gemelas
bed clothes la ropa de cama
bedroom el dormitorio
bee la abeja
beech la haya
beef la ternera
beer la cerveza
beetroot la remolacha
before antes de
  before breakfast antes de desayunar
beggar el/la mendigo(a)
to begin empezar
behind detrás de
  behind the house detrás de la casa
beige beige
to believe creer
bell (church) la campana ; (door bell) el timbre
below debajo
belt el cinturón
bend (in road) la curva

berth (plane, train, ship) la litera
beside (next to) al lado de
  beside the bank al lado del banco
best el/la mejor
to bet on apostar por
better mejor
  better than mejor que
between entre
bib el babero
bicycle la bicicleta
  by bicycle en bicicleta
bicycle lock el candado de la bicicleta
bicycle repair kit la caja de herramientas
bidet el bidet
big grande
  bigger than mayor que
bike (pushbike) la bicicleta
  mountain bike la bicicleta de montaña
bikini el bikini
bilberry el arándano
bill la factura ; (in restaurant) la cuenta
billion un billón
bin el cubo
bin liner la bolsa de la basura
binoculars los prismáticos
bird el pájaro
biro el bolígrafo
birth certificate la partida de nacimiento
birthday el cumpleaños
  happy birthday! ¡feliz cumpleaños!
  my birthday is on ... mi cumpleaños es el...
birthday card la tarjeta de cumpleaños
birthday present el regalo de cumpleaños
biscuits las galletas
bit: *a bit of* un poco de
to bite morder ; (insect) picar

b

bitten *(by animal)* mordido(a)
(by insect) picado(a)
bitter *(taste)* amargo(a)
black negro(a)
blackberry la mora
blackcurrant la grosella negra
black ice la capa invisible de
hielo en la carretera
blanket la manta
bleach *(household)* la lejía
to bleed sangrar
blender *(for food)* la licuadora
blind *(person)* ciego(a)
blind *(for window)* la persiana
blister la ampolla
blocked *(road)* cortado(a)
(pipe) obstruido(a)
blond *(person)* rubio(a)
blood la sangre
blood group el grupo sanguíneo
blood pressure la presión
sanguínea
blood test el análisis de sangre
blouse la blusa
blow-dry el secado a mano
blue azul
dark blue azul marino
light blue azul claro
blunt *(knife, blade)* desafilado(a)
boar el cerdo
boarding card/pass la tarjeta de
embarque
boat *(large)* el barco
(small) la barca
boat trip la excursión en barco
to boil hervir
boiled hervido(a)
bomb la bomba
bone el hueso
(fish bone) la espina
bonfire la hoguera
bonnet *(car)* el capó
book el libro
to book reservar
booking la reserva

booking office *(train)* el despacho
de billetes
bookshop la librería
boot *(car)* el maletero
boots las botas
(short) los botines
border *(of country)* la frontera
boring aburrido(a)
born: I was born on... nací en...
to borrow pedir prestado
boss el/la jefe(a)
both ambos(as)
bottle la botella
a bottle of wine una botella de
vino
a half-bottle media botella
bottle opener el abrebotellas
bottom *(of pool, garden)* el fondo
(bum) el culo
bowl *(for soup, etc)* el tazón
bow tie la pajarita
box la caja
box office *(theatre)* la taquilla
boxer shorts los calzoncillos
boy el chico
boyfriend el novio
bra el sujetador
bracelet la pulsera
brake el freno
to brake frenar
brake fluid el líquido de frenos
brake light la luz de freno
branch *(of tree)* la rama
(of bank, etc) la sucursal
brand *(make)* la marca
brandy el coñac
brass el latón
brave valiente
bread el pan
wholemeal bread el pan integral
french bread la barra de pan
sliced bread el pan de molde
breadcrumbs el pan rallado
bread roll el panecillo
to break romper

breakable frágil
breakdown *(car)* la avería
(*nervous*) la crisis nerviosa
breakdown van la grúa
breakfast el desayuno
breast *(of chicken)* la pechuga
to breathe respirar
brick el ladrillo
bride la novia
bridegroom el novio
bridge el puente
(*game*) el bridge
briefcase la cartera
Brillo pads® las nanas®
to bring traer
Britain Gran Bretaña
British británico(a)
broccoli el brécol ; el brócoli
brochure el folleto
broken roto(a)
my leg is broken me he
fracturado la pierna
broken down *(car, etc)* averiado(a)
bronchitis la bronquitis
bronze el bronce
brooch el broche
broom *(brush)* la escoba
brother el hermano
brother-in-law el cuñado
brown marrón
bruise el moretón ; el cardenal
brush el cepillo
Brussels sprouts las coles de
Bruselas
bubble bath el baño de espuma
bucket el cubo
buffet car el coche-comedor
to build construir
building el edificio
bulb *(electric)* la bombilla
bull el toro
bullfight la corrida de toros
bullfighter el torero ; el matador
bullring la plaza de toros
bumbag la riñonera

bumper *(on car)* el parachoques
bunch *(of flowers)* el ramo
(*grapes*) el racimo
bungee jumping el bunyi
bureau de change la oficina de
cambio
burger la hamburguesa
burglar el/la ladrón(a)
to burn quemar
burnt *(food)* quemado(a)
bus el autobús *[Mexico el camión]*
bus pass el bonobús
bus station la estación de
autobuses
bus stop la parada de autobús
bus ticket el billete de autobús
business el negocio
on business de negocios
business address la dirección del
trabajo
business card la tarjeta de visita
business class la clase preferente
businessman/woman el
hombre/la mujer de negocios
business trip el viaje de negocios
busy ocupado(a)
but pero
butcher's la carnicería
butter la mantequilla
butterfly la mariposa
button el botón
to buy comprar
by *(via)* por
(*beside*) al lado de
by bus en autobús
by car en coche
by train en tren
bypass *(road)* la carretera de
circunvalación

C

cab *(taxi)* el taxi
cabaret el cabaret
cabbage la col

cabin *(on boat)* el camarote
cablecar el teleférico
cable TV la televisión por cable
café el café
  internet café el café internet
cafetière la cafetera
cake *(big)* la tarta
  (little) el pastel
cake shop la pastelería
calculator la calculadora
calendar el calendario
calf *(young cow)* el becerro
call *(telephone)* la llamada
  a long distance call una
  conferencia
to call *(phone)* llamar por teléfono
calm tranquilo(a)
camcorder la vídeocámara
camera la máquina de fotos ; la
  cámara
camera case el estuche de la
  cámara
camera shop la tienda de
  fotografía
to camp acampar
camping gas el cámping gas
camping stove el hornillo de gas
campsite el cámping
can la lata
to can *(to be able)* poder *see*
  GRAMMAR
can opener el abrelatas
Canada el Canadá
Canadian canadiense
canal el canal
to cancel anular; cancelar
cancellation la cancelación
cancer el cáncer
candle la vela
canoe la canoa
cap *(hat)* la gorra
  (diaphragm) el diafragma
capital *(city)* la capital
cappuccino el capuchino
car el coche *[Lat. Am. el carro]*

car alarm la alarma de coche
car ferry el transbordador ; el
  ferry
car hire el alquiler de coches
car insurance el seguro del coche
car keys las llaves del coche
car park el aparcamiento
  [Lat. Am. el estacionamiento]
car radio la radio del coche
car seat *(for children)* el asiento
  para niños
car wash el lavado (automático)
  de coches
carafe la jarra
caravan la caravana
carburettor el carburador
card *(greetings, business)* la tarjeta
  playing cards las cartas
cardboard el cartón
cardigan la chaqueta de punto
careful cuidadoso(a)
  be careful! ¡ten cuidado!
carnation el clavel
carpet *(rug)* la alfombra
  (fitted) la moqueta
carriage *(railway)* el vagón
carrot la zanahoria
to carry llevar
carving knife el cuchillo de trinchar
case *(suitcase)* la maleta
cash el dinero en efectivo
to cash *(cheque)* cobrar
cash desk la caja
cash dispenser el cajero
  automático
cashier el/la cajero(a)
casino el casino
casserole el guiso ; la cazuela
cassette el casete
cassette player el radiocasete
castanets las castañuelas
castle el castillo
casualty department urgencias
cat el gato
catalogue el catálogo

to catch (bus, train, etc.) coger [Lat. Am. tomar]
cathedral la catedral
Catholic católico(a)
cauliflower la coliflor
cave la cueva
CD el CD
CD player el lector de CD
ceiling el techo
celery el apio
cellar la bodega
cemetery el cementerio
centimetre el centímetro
central central
central heating la calefacción central
central locking (car) el cierre centralizado
centre el centro
century el siglo
19th century el siglo XIX
21st century el siglo XXI
ceramic la cerámica
certain (sure) seguro(a)
certificate el certificado
chain la cadena
chair la silla
chairlift el telesilla
chalet el chalé ; el chalet
chambermaid la camarera
Champagne el champán
change el cambio
(small coins) suelto
(money returned) la vuelta
to change cambiar
to change money cambiar dinero
to change (clothes) cambiarse
to change (train) hacer transbordo
changing room el probador
Channel (English) el Canal de la Mancha
chapel la capilla
charcoal el carbón vegetal
charter flight el vuelo chárter

cheap barato(a)
cheaper más barato(a)
cheap rate la tarifa baja
to check revisar ; comprobar
to check in (at airport) facturar el equipaje
(at hotel) registrarse
check-in la facturación
cheek la mejilla
cheers! ¡salud!
cheese el queso
cheeseburger la hamburguesa con queso
chef el chef
chemist's la farmacia
cheque el talón ; el cheque
cheque book el talonario
cheque card la tarjeta bancaria
cherry la cereza
chest (anat.) el pecho
chest of drawers la cómoda
chestnut la castaña
chewing gum el chicle
chicken el pollo
chickenpox la varicela
chickpea el garbanzo
child (boy) el niño
(girl) la niña
children (infants) los niños
for children para niños
child safety seat (car) el asiento para niños
chilli la guindilla ; el chile
chimney la chimenea
chin la barbilla
china la porcelana
chips las patatas fritas
chives los cebollinos
chocolate el chocolate
chocolates los bombones
choir el coro
chop (meat) la chuleta
chopping board la tabla de cortar
christening el bautizo

C

Christmas la Navidad
merry Christmas! ¡feliz navidad!
Christmas card la tarjeta de navidad
Christmas Eve la Nochebuena
Christmas present el regalo de navidad
chrysanthemum el crisantemo
church la iglesia
cider la sidra
cigar el puro
cigarette el cigarrillo
cigarette lighter el mechero
cigarette papers el papel de fumar
cinema el cine
circle *(theatre)* el anfiteatro
circuit breaker el cortacircuitos
circus el circo
cistern la cisterna
citizen el/la ciudadano(a)
city la ciudad
city centre el centro de la ciudad
class: *first class* primera clase
second class segunda clase
clean limpio(a)
to clean limpiar
cleanser *(for face)* el desmaquillador
clear claro(a)
client el/la cliente
cliff *(along coast)* el acantilado
(in mountains) el precipicio
to climb *(mountains)* escalar
climbing boots las botas de escalar
clingfilm® el rollo de plástico
clinic la clínica
cloakroom el guardarropa
clock el reloj
to close cerrar
closed *(shop, etc)* cerrado(a)
cloth *(rag)* el trapo
(fabric) la tela ; el paño
clothes la ropa

clothes line el tendedero
clothes peg la pinza
clothes shop la tienda de ropa
cloudy nublado(a)
clove *(spice)* el clavo
club el club
clutch *(in car)* el embrague
coach *(bus)* el autocar
coach station la estación de autobuses
coach trip la excursión en autocar
coal el carbón
coast la costa
coastguard el/la guardacostas
coat el abrigo
coat hanger la percha
Coca cola® la Coca Cola®
cockroach la cucaracha
cocktail el cóctel
cocoa el cacao
coconut el coco
cod el bacalao
code el código
coffee el café
black coffee el café solo
white coffee el café con leche
cappuccino el capuchino
decaffeinated coffee el café descafeinado
coil *(IUD)* el DIU
coin la moneda
Coke® la Coca Cola®
colander el colador
cold frío(a)
I'm cold tengo frío
it's cold hace frío
cold water el agua fría
cold *(illness)* el resfriado
I have a cold estoy resfriado(a)
cold sore la calentura
collar el cuello
collar bone la clavícula
colleague el/la colega
to collect recoger

colour el color
colour-blind daltónico(a)
colour film *(for camera)* el carrete en color
comb el peine
to come venir
(to arrive) llegar
to come back volver
to come in entrar
come in! ¡pase! [Lat. Am. ¡siga!]
comedy la comedia
comfortable cómodo(a)
company *(firm)* la empresa
compartment el compartimento
compass la brújula
to complain reclamar
complaint la reclamación ; la queja
composer el/la compositor(a)
compulsory obligatorio(a)
computer el ordenador
computer disk *(floppy)* el disquete
computer game el juego de ordenador
computer program el programa de ordenador
computer software el software
concert el concierto
concert hall la sala de conciertos
concession el descuento
concussion la conmoción cerebral
conditioner el suavizante
condom el condón
conductor *(on bus)* el/la cobrador(a)
conference el congreso
to confirm confirmar
please confirm por favor, confirme
confirmation *(flight, booking)* la confirmación
congratulations! ¡enhorabuena!
connection *(train, etc.)* el enlace
constipated estreñido(a)
consulate el consulado

to contact ponerse en contacto
contact lens la lentilla
contact lens cleaner la solución limpiadora para lentillas
to continue continuar
contraceptive el anticonceptivo
contract el contrato
convenient: *is it convenient?* ¿le viene bien?
to cook cocinar
cooked preparado(a)
cooker la cocina
cool fresco(a)
cool-box la nevera portátil
copper el cobre
copy *(duplicate)* la copia ; *(of book)* el ejemplar
to copy copiar
coral el coral
coriander el cilantro
cork el corcho
corkscrew el sacacorchos
corner la esquina
corridor el pasillo
cortisone la cortisona
cost *(price)* el precio
to cost costar
how much does it cost? ¿cuánto cuesta?
cot la cuna
cottage la casita de campo
cotton el algodón
cotton buds los bastoncillos
cotton wool el algodón
couchette la litera
to cough toser
cough la tos
cough mixture el jarabe para la tos
cough sweets los caramelos para la tos
counter *(in shop)* el mostrador *(in bar)* la barra
country *(not town)* el campo *(nation)* el país

C

C

countryside el campo
couple *(2 people)* la pareja
courgette el calabacín
courier *(tour guide)* el/la guía de turismo
courier service el servicio de mensajero
course *(of study)* el curso
(of meal) el plato
cousin el/la primo(a)
cover charge *(in restaurant)* el cubierto
cow la vaca
crab el cangrejo
crafts la artesanía
craftsman/woman el/la artesano(a)
cramps los calambres
crash *(car)* el accidente
to crash *(car)* chocar
crash helmet el casco protector
cream *(lotion)* la crema
(on milk) la nata
soured cream la nata cortada
whipped cream la nata montada
credit card la tarjeta de crédito
crime el delito
crisps las patatas fritas; las patatas chips
croissant el croissant
cross *(crucifix)* la cruz
to cross *(road)* cruzar
cross country skiing el esquí de fondo
crossing *(sea)* la travesía
crossroads el cruce
crossword puzzle el crucigrama
crowded concurrido(a)
crown la corona
cruise el crucero
crutches las muletas
to cry *(weep)* llorar
crystal el cristal
cucumber el pepino
cufflinks los gemelos
cul-de-sac el callejón sin salida

cumin el comino
cup la taza
cupboard el armario
currant la pasa
currency la moneda
current *(air, water, etc)* la corriente
curtain la cortina
cushion el cojín
custard las natillas
custom *(tradition)* la costumbre
customer el/la cliente
customs *(control)* la aduana
cut el corte
to cut cortar
cutlery los cubiertos
to cycle ir en bicicleta
cycle track el carril de bicicleta
cyst el quiste
cystitis la cistitis

D

daffodil el narciso
dahlia la dalia
daily *(each day)* cada día; diario
dairy produce los productos lácteos
daisy la margarita
damage los daños
damp húmedo(a)
dance el baile
to dance bailar
danger el peligro
dangerous peligroso(a)
dark oscuro(a)
after dark por la noche
date la fecha
date of birth la fecha de nacimiento
daughter la hija
daughter-in-law la cuñada
dawn el amanecer
day el día
every day todos los días
per day al día

dead muerto(a)
deaf sordo(a)
dear *(on letter)* querido(a)
 (expensive) caro(a)
debt la deuda
decaffeinated coffee el café descafeinado
 have you decaff? ¿tiene café descafeinado?
December diciembre
deck chair la tumbona
to declare: *nothing to declare* nada que declarar
deep profundo(a)
deep freeze el ultracongelador
to defrost descongelar
to de-ice descongelar
delay el retraso
 how long is the delay? ¿cuánto lleva de retraso?
delayed retrasado(a)
delicatessen la charcutería
delicious delicioso(a)
dental floss la seda dental
dentist el/la dentista
dentures la dentadura postiza
deodorant el desodorante
department store los grandes almacenes
departure la salida
departure lounge la sala de embarque
departures las salidas
deposit la fianza
to describe describir
description la descripción
desk *(in hotel, airport)* el mostrador
dessert el postre
details los detalles
 (personal) los datos personales
detour el desvío
to develop *(photos)* revelar
diabetes la diabetes
diabetic diabético(a)

I'm diabetic soy diabético(a)
to dial marcar
dialling code el prefijo
dialling tone el tono de marcar
diamond el diamante
diapers los pañales
diarrhoea la diarrea
diary la agenda
dice los dados
dictionary el diccionario
to die morir
diesel el gasoil ; el gasóleo
diet la dieta
 I'm on a diet estoy a dieta
different distinto(a)
difficult difícil
dinghy el bote
dining room el comedor
dinner *(evening meal)* la cena
 to have dinner cenar
diplomat el/la diplomático(a)
direct *(train, etc)* directo(a)
directions *(instructions)* las instrucciones
 to ask for directions preguntar el camino
directory *(phone)* la guía telefónica
directory enquiries la información telefónica
dirty sucio(a)
disabled minusválido(a)
to disappear desaparecer
disaster el desastre
disco la discoteca
discount el descuento
to discover descubrir
disease la enfermedad
dish el plato
dishtowel el paño de cocina
dishwasher el lavavajillas
dishwasher powder el detergente para lavavajillas
disinfectant el desinfectante
disk *(computer)* el disco
 floppy disk el disquete

d

hard disk el disco duro
to dislocate *(joint)* dislocarse
distant distante ; lejano(a)
distilled water el agua destilada
district el barrio
to disturb molestar
to dive tirarse al agua
diversion el desvío
divorced divorciado(a)
  I'm divorced estoy divorciado(a)
DIY shop la tienda de bricolaje
dizzy mareado(a)
to do hacer *see* **GRAMMAR**
doctor el/la médico(a)
documents los documentos
dog el perro
dog lead la correa del perro
doll la muñeca
dollar el dólar
domestic *(flight)* nacional
dominoes el dominó

d

donor card la tarjeta de donante
donut el buñuelo
door la puerta
doorbell el timbre
double doble
double bed la cama de matrimonio
double room la habitación doble
doughnut el buñuelo
down: *to go down* bajar
downstairs abajo
dragonfly la libélula
drain el desagüe
draught *(of air)* la corriente
  there's a draught hay corriente
draught lager la cerveza de barril
drawer el cajón
drawing el dibujo
dress el vestido

d

to dress *(to get dressed)* vestirse
dressing *(for food)* el aliño
dressing gown la bata
drill *(tool)* la taladradora
drink la bebida

to drink beber
drinking chocolate el chocolate caliente
drinking water el agua potable
to drive conducir
  [Lat. Am. manejar]
driver *(of car)* el/la conductor(a)
driving licence el carné de conducir
drought la sequía
to drown ahogarse
drug la droga
  (medicine) la medicina
drunk borracho(a)
dry seco(a)
to dry secar
dry-cleaner's la tintorería ; la limpieza en seco
dryer la secadora
duck el pato
due: *when is it due?* ¿para cuándo está previsto?
dummy *(for baby)* el chupete
during durante
dust el polvo
duster el trapo del polvo
dustpan and brush el mini cepillo y recogedor
duty-free libre de impuesto
duty-free shop la tienda libre de impuestos
duvet el edredón
duvet cover la funda de edredón
dye el tinte
dynamo la dinamo

E

each cada
eagle el águila
ear *(outside)* la oreja ; *(inside)* el oído
earache el dolor de oídos
  I have earache me duele el oído
earphones los auriculares

earrings los pendientes
earlier antes
early temprano
earth la tierra
earthquake el terremoto
east el este
Easter la Pascua ; la Semana Santa
Easter egg el huevo de pascua
easy fácil
to eat comer
ebony el ébano
eel la anguila
egg el huevo
  fried egg el huevo frito
  hard-boiled egg el huevo duro
  scrambled eggs los huevos revueltos
  soft-boiled egg el huevo pasado por agua
egg white la clara
egg yolk la yema
either... or... o...o...
elastic band la goma
elastoplast la tirita
elbow el codo
electrician el/la electricista
electricity la electricidad
electricity meter el contador de electricidad
electric razor la maquinilla de afeitar eléctica
electric shock el calambre
elevator el ascensor
e-mail el correo electrónico
e-mail address la dirección de correo electrónico
embassy la embajada
emergency la emergencia
emergency exit la salida de emergencia; la salida de socorro
empty vacío(a)
end el fin
engaged *(to marry)* prometido(a)
  (toilet, phone) ocupado(a)

engine el motor
engineer el/la ingeniero(a)
England Inglaterra
English inglés(a)
  (language) el inglés
to enjoy *(to like)* gustar
  I enjoy swimming me gusta nadar
  I enjoy dancing me gusta bailar
  enjoy your meal! ¡que aproveche!
  to enjoy oneself divertirse
enough bastante
  that's enough ya basta
enquiry desk la información
to enter entrar en
enthusiastic entusiasta
entrance la entrada
entrance fee el precio de entrada
envelope el sobre
epileptic epiléptico(a)
epileptic fit el ataque epiléptico
equipment el equipo
eraser la goma (de borrar)
escalator la escalera mecánica
to escape escapar
espadrilles las alpargatas
essential imprescindible
estate agent's la agencia inmobiliaria
Euro Euro
Eurocheque el Eurocheque
Europe Europa
European Union la Unión europea
eve la víspera
  Christmas Eve La Nochebuena
  New Year's Eve La Nochevieja
even *(number)* par
evening la tarde
  this evening esta tarde
  tomorrow evening mañana por la tarde
  in the evening por la tarde
evening dress el traje de etiqueta
evening meal la cena
every cada
everyone todo el mundo

e

e everything todo
everywhere en todas partes
examination el examen
example: *for example* por ejemplo
excellent excelente
except excepto ; salvo
excess luggage el exceso de equipaje
exchange el cambio
to exchange cambiar
exchange rate el tipo de cambio
exciting emocionante
excursion la excursión
excuse me! perdón
exercise *(physical)* el ejercicio
exercise book el cuaderno
exhaust pipe el tubo de escape
exhibition la exposición
exit la salida
expenses los gastos
expensive caro(a)
expert el/la experto(a)

e to expire *(ticket, passport)* caducar
to explain explicar
explosion la explosión
to export exportar
express *(train)* el rápido ; el expreso
express: *to send a letter express* enviar una carta por correo urgente
extension *(electrical)* el alargador
extra *(in addition)* de más *(more)* adicional
eye el ojo
eyebrows las cejas
eye drops el colirio
eyelashes las pestañas
eyeliner el lápiz de ojos

F

f fabric la tela; el tejido
face la cara
face cloth la toallita

facial la limpieza de cutis
factory la fábrica
to faint desmayarse
fainted desmayado(a)
fair *(hair)* rubio(a)
fair *(funfair)* el parque de atracciones
fairway *(golf)* la calle
fake falso(a)
fall *(autumn)* el otoño
to fall caer ; caerse
he/she has fallen se ha caído
false teeth la dentadura postiza
family la familia
famous famoso(a)
fan *(electric)* el ventilador *(hand-held)* el abanico *(football, etc)* el/la hincha *(jazz, etc)* el/la aficionado(a)
fan belt la correa del ventilador
far lejos
is it far? ¿está lejos?
how far is it? ¿a cuánto está?
farm la granja
farmer el/la granjero(a)
farmhouse la granja
fashionable de moda
fast rápido(a)
too fast demasiado rápido
to fasten *(seatbelt, etc)* abrocharse
fat gordo(a)
father el padre
father-in-law el suegro
fault *(defect)* el defecto
favourite favorito(a) ; preferido(a)
to fax mandar por fax
fax el fax
by fax por fax
fax number el número de fax
feather la pluma
February febrero
to feed dar de comer
to feel sentir
I don't feel well no me siento bien

feet los pies
felt-tip pen el rotulador
female mujer
ferry el transbordador
festival el festival
to fetch (to bring) traer
  (to go and get) ir a buscar
fever la fiebre
few pocos(as)
  a few algunos(as)
fiancé(e) el/la novio(a)
field el campo
fig el higo
to fight luchar
file (computer) el fichero
  (nail) la lima
to fill llenar
  (to fill in form) rellenar
  fill it up, please! (car) lleno, por favor
fillet el filete
filling (in tooth) el empaste
film (at cinema) la película
  (for camera) el carrete
  colour film el carrete en color
  black and white film el carrete en blanco y negro
Filofax® la agenda
filter el filtro
to find encontrar
fine (to be paid) la multa
finger el dedo
to finish acabar
fir el abeto
fire el fuego ; el incendio
  fire! ¡fuego!
fire alarm la alarma de incendios
fire brigade los bomberos
fire engine el coche de bomberos
fire escape la salida de incendios
fire extinguisher el extintor
fireplace la chimenea
fireworks los fuegos artificiales
first primero(a)

first aid los primeros auxilios
first aid kit el botiquín de primeros auxilios
first class de primera clase
first floor el primer piso
first name el nombre de pila
fish el pescado
to fish pescar
fisherman/woman el/la pescador(a)
fishing permit la licencia de pesca
fishing rod la caña de pescar
fishmonger's la pescadería
fit (seizure) el ataque
to fit (clothes) quedar bien
  it doesn't fit me no es mi talla
to fix arreglar
  can you fix it? ¿puede arreglarlo?
fizzy con gas
flag la bandera
flannel (face cloth) la manopla
flash (for camera) el flash
flashlight la linterna
flask (thermos) el termo
flat (apartment) el piso
flat llano(a)
  (battery) descargado(a)
  (beer) sin gas
  it's flat ya no tiene gas
flat tyre la rueda pinchada
flavour el sabor
  which flavour? ¿qué sabor?
flaw el defecto
fleas las pulgas
fleece (top/jacket) el forro polar
flex el cable eléctrico
flight el vuelo
flip flops las chancletas
flippers las aletas
flood la inundación
  flash flood la riada
floor (of building) la planta
  (of room) el suelo
  which floor? ¿qué planta?

f

111

f *ground floor* la planta baja
floorcloth el trapo de piso
floppy disk el disquete
florist's shop la floristería
flour la harina
flower la flor
flu la gripe
fly la mosca
to fly volar
fly sheet el doble techo
foggy: *it's foggy* hay niebla
foil *(tinfoil)* el papel albal®
to fold doblar
to follow seguir
food la comida
food poisoning la intoxicación
  por alimentos
foot el pie
  on foot a pie
football el fútbol
football match el partido de fútbol
football pitch el campo de fútbol
football player el/la futbolista
footpath *(in country)* la vereda ;
  el sendero
for para
  for me para mi
  for you para usted
  for him/her/us para
  él/ella/nosotros
forbidden prohibido(a)
forehead la frente
foreign extranjero(a)
foreigner el extranjero(a)
forest el bosque
forever para siempre
to forget olvidar
fork *(for eating)* el tenedor
  (in road) la bifurcación
form *(document)* el impreso
formal dress el traje de etiqueta
fortnight quince días ; la quincena
forward adelante
foul *(football)* la falta
fountain la fuente

four-wheel drive la tracción a
  cuatro ruedas
fox el zorro
fracture la fractura
fragile frágil
frame *(picture)* el marco
France Francia
free *(not occupied)* libre
  (costing nothing) gratis
freezer el congelador
French francés/francesa
  (language) el francés
french beans las judías verdes
french fries las patatas fritas
frequent frecuente
fresh fresco(a)
fresh water el agua dulce
Friday el viernes
fridge el frigorífico
fried frito(a)
friend el/la amigo(a)
frisbee® el platillo volante
frog la rana
frogs' legs las ancas de rana
from de ; desde
  from Scotland de Escocia
  from England de Inglaterra
front la parte delantera
  in front of delante de
front door la puerta de la calle
frost la helada
frozen congelado(a)
fruit la fruta
  dried fruit la fruta seca
fruit juice el zumo (de fruta)
fruit salad la ensalada de frutas ;
  la macedonia
to fry freír
frying pan la sartén
fuel *(petrol)* la gasolina
fuel gauge el indicador de la
  gasolina
fuel tank el depósito de gasolina
full lleno(a)
  (occupied) ocupado(a)

full board pensión completa
fumes (of car) los gases
fun la diversión
funeral el funeral
funfair el parque de atracciones
funny (amusing) divertido(a)
fur la piel
fur coat el abrigo de piel
furnished amueblado(a)
furniture los muebles
fuse el fusible
fuse box la caja de fusibles
futon el futón
future el futuro

G

gallery la galería
gallon = approx. 4.5 litres
game el juego
  (animal) la caza
garage el garaje
  (for repairs) el taller
garden el jardín
gardener el/la jardinero(a)
garlic el ajo
gas el gas
gas cooker la cocina de gas
gas cylinder la bombona de gas
gastritis la gastritis
gate (airport) la puerta
gay (person) gay
gear la marcha
  first gear la primera
  second gear la segunda
  third gear la tercera
  fourth gear la cuarta
  neutral el punto muerto
  reverse la marcha atrás
gearbox la caja de cambios
generous generoso(a)
gents (toilet) los servicios de
  caballeros
genuine auténtico(a)
geranium el geranio

German alemán/alemana
  (language) el alemán
German measles la rubeola
Germany Alemania
to get (to obtain) conseguir
  (to receive) recibir
  (to bring) traer
to get in (vehicle) entrar (en) ;
  subir (al)
to get out (bus, car, train) bajarse
  de
gift el regalo
gift shop la tienda de regalos
gin and tonic el gin-tonic
ginger (spice) el jengibre
girl la chica
girlfriend la novia
to give dar
to give back devolver
glacier el glaciar
glass (for drinking) el vaso
  (substance) el cristal
  a glass of water un vaso de agua
  a glass of wine un vaso de vino
glasses (spectacles) las gafas
  [Lat. Am. los lentes]
glasses case la funda de gafas
gloves los guantes
glue el pegamento
to go ir
  I'm going to ... voy a...
  we're going to ... vamos a...
  to go home irse a casa
to go back volver
to go down(stairs) bajar
to go in entrar (en)
to go out salir
goat la cabra
God Dios
goggles (for swimming) las gafas
  de natación
  (for skiing) las gafas de esquí
gold el oro
golf el golf
golf ball la pelota de golf
golf clubs los palos de golf

113

g golf course el campo de golf
good bueno(a)
   very good muy bueno
good afternoon buenas tardes
goodbye adiós
good day buenos días
good evening buenas tardes ;
   (later) buenas noches
good morning buenos días
good night buenas noches
goose el ganso
gooseberry la grosella espinosa
Gothic Gótico(a)
gram(me) el gramo
granddaughter la nieta
grandfather el abuelo
grandmother la abuela
grandparents los abuelos
grandson el nieto
grapefruit el pomelo
grapefruit juice el zumo de
   pomelo

g grapes la uva
   green/black grapes las uvas
   verdes/negras
grass la hierba
grated *(cheese, etc)* rallado(a)
grater *(for cheese, etc)* el rallador
greasy grasiento(a)
great *(big)* grande
Great Britain Gran Bretaña
green verde
green card la carta verde
greengrocer's la frutería
greetings card la tarjeta de
   felicitación
grey gris
grill hacer al grill
   (barbecue) la parrilla
to grill gratinar
   (in barbecue) asar a la parrilla
g grilled gratinado(a)
   (in barbecue) a la parrilla
grocer's la tienda de
   alimentación

ground el suelo
ground floor la planta baja
   on the ground floor en la planta
   baja
groundsheet la tela impermeable
group el grupo
to grow *(cultivate)* cultivar
guarantee la garantía
guest el/la invitado(a)
   (in hotel) el/la huésped
guesthouse la pensión
guide *(tour guide)* el/la guía
to guide guiar
guidebook la guía turística
guided tour la visita con guía
guitar la guitarra
gun la pistola
gym shoes las zapatillas de
   deporte

H

haberdasher's la mercería
haddock el abadejo
haemorrhoids las hemorroides
hail el granizo
hair el pelo
hairbrush el cepillo del pelo
haircut el corte de pelo
hairdresser el/la peluquero(a)
hairdryer el secador de pelo
hair dye el tinte de pelo
hair gel el gel
hairgrip la horquilla
hair mousse la espuma del pelo
hair spray la laca
hake la merluza
half medio(a)
   half an hour media hora
half board media pensión
half-price a mitad de precio
ham el jamón
   (cooked) el jamón de York
   (cured) el jamón serrano

hamburger la hamburguesa
hammer el martillo
hand la mano
handbag el bolso
hand luggage el equipaje de mano
hand-made hecho(a) a mano
handicapped minusválido(a)
handkerchief el pañuelo
handle *(of cup)* el asa
(of door) el picaporte
handlebars el manillar
handsome guapo(a)
to hang up *(phone)* colgar
hanger *(coat hanger)* la percha
hang gliding el vuelo con ala delta
hangover la resaca
to happen pasar
what happened? ¿qué ha pasado?
happy feliz
happy birthday! ¡feliz cumpleanos!
harbour el puerto
hard duro(a)
(difficult) difícil
hard disk el disco duro
hardware shop la ferretería
hare la liebre
harvest la cosecha
hat el sombrero
to have tener *see* **GRAMMAR**
I have ... tengo
I don't have ... no tengo...
we have ... tenemos...
we don't have ... no tenemos...
do you have ...? ¿tiene...?
to have to tener que
hay fever la alergia al polen
hazelnut la avellana
he él *see* **GRAMMAR**
head la cabeza
headache el dolor de cabeza
I have a headache me duele la cabeza

headlights los faros
headphones los auriculares
head waiter el maître
health food shop la tienda de dietética
to hear oír
hearing aid el audífono
heart el corazón
heart attack el infarto; el ataque cardíaco
heartburn el ardor de estómago
to heat up *(milk, food)* calentar
heater el calentador
heating la calefacción
heaven el cielo
heavy pesado(a)
heel *(of foot)* el talón
(of shoe) el tacón
height la altura
helicopter el helicóptero
hello hola
(on phone) diga
helmet *(for bike, etc)* el casco
help! socorro
to help ayudar
can you help me? ¿puede ayudarme?
hem el dobladillo
hen la gallina
hepatitis la hepatitis
her su
herb la hierba
herbal tea la infusión (de hierbas)
here aquí
here is ... aquí tiene...
here is my passport aquí tiene mi pasaporte
hernia la hernia
hi! hola
to hide *(something)* esconder
(oneself) esconderse
high alto(a)
high blood pressure la tensión alta
high chair la silla alta para los niños

h

high tide la marea alta
hill la colina
hill-walking el montañismo
hip la cadera
hip replacement la prótesis de cadera
hire (bike, boat, etc) el alquiler
  car hire el alquiler de coches
to hire alquilar
his su
historic histórico(a)
history la historia
to hit pegar
to hitchhike hacer auto-stop
HIV el virus del sida
HIV positive seropositivo(a)
hobby el hobby ; el pasatiempo
to hold tener
  (to contain) contener
hold-up (traffic jam) el atasco
hole el agujero
holiday las vacaciones
  (public) la fiesta
  on holiday de vacaciones
holy santo(a)
home la casa
  at home en casa
homeopathy la homeopatía
homesick: to be homesick tener morriña
  I'm homesick tengo morriña
homosexual homosexual
honest sincero(a)
honey la miel
honeymoon la luna de miel
hood (jacket) la capucha
hook (fishing) el anzuelo
to hope esperar
  I hope so/not espero que sí/no
horn (car) el claxon ; la bocina
hors d'oeuvre los entremeses
horse el caballo
horse racing las carreras de caballos ; la hípica
hosepipe la manguera

hospital el hospital
hostel el hostal
hot caliente
  I'm hot tengo calor
  it's hot (weather) hace calor
  hot water el agua caliente
hot chocolate el chocolate caliente
hot-water bottle la botella de agua caliente
hotel el hotel
hour la hora
  half an hour media hora
house la casa
housewife/husband la/el ama(o) de casa
house wine el vino de la casa
housework las tareas domésticas
hovercraft el aerodeslizador ; el "hovercraft"
how (in what way) cómo
  how much? ¿cuánto?
  how many? ¿cuántos?
  how are you? ¿cómo está?
hundred cien
  five hundred quinientos(as)
hungry: to be hungry tengo hambre
to hunt cazar
hunting permit el permiso de caza
hurry: I'm in a hurry tengo prisa
to hurt (injure) hacer daño
  my back hurts me duele la espalda
  that hurts eso duele
husband el marido
hut (bathing/beach) la caseta
  (mountain) el refugio
hydrofoil el hidrofoil ; el hidrodeslizador
hypodermic needle la aguja hipodérmica

I

I yo see **GRAMMAR**
ice el hielo
  (cube) el cubito
  with ice con hielo
ice box la nevera
icecream el helado
ice lolly el polo
ice rink la pista de patinaje
to ice skate patinar sobre hielo
ice tea el té frío
idea la idea
identity card el carné de identidad
if si
ignition el encendido
ignition key la llave de contacto
ill enfermo(a)
  I'm ill estoy enfermo(a)
immediately inmediatamente ; en seguida
immersion heater el calentador eléctrico
immunisation la inmunización
important importante
impossible: *it's impossible* es imposible
in dentro de ; en
  in 10 minutes dentro de 10 minutos
  in London en Londres
in front of delante de
inch la pulgada = approx. 2.5 cm
included incluido(a)
to increase aumentar
indicator *(in car)* el intermitente
indigestion la indigestión
indigestion tablets las pastillas para la indigestión
indoors dentro
  (at home) en casa
infection la infección
infectious contagioso(a)
information la información

ingredients los ingredientes
inhaler *(for medication)* el inhalador
injection la inyección
to injure herir
injured herido(a)
injury la herida
ink la tinta
inn la pensión
inner tube la cámara
insect el insecto
insect bite la picadura de insecto
insect repellent la loción contra insectos
inside dentro de
instant coffee el café instantáneo
instead of en lugar de
instructor el/la instructor(a)
insulin la insulina
insurance el seguro
insurance certificate el certificado de seguros
to insure asegurar
insured asegurado(a)
intelligent inteligente
interesting interesante
international internacional
internet el internet
  internet café el café internet
interpreter el/la intérprete
interval *(theatre, etc)* el descanso; el intermedio
interview la entrevista
into en
  into town al centro
to introduce to presentar a
invitation la invitación
to invite invitar
invoice la factura
Ireland Irlanda
Irish irlandés/irlandesa
iron *(for clothes)* la plancha
  (metal) el hierro
to iron planchar
ironing board la tabla de planchar
ironmonger's la ferretería

is *see* (to be) **GRAMMAR**
island la isla
it lo/la *see* **GRAMMAR**
Italian italiano(a)
  (language) el italiano
Italy Italia
itch el picor
to itch picar
item el artículo
itemized bill la factura detallada
ivory el marfil

J

jack *(for car)* el gato
jacket la chaqueta
  waterproof jacket la chaqueta impermeable
jacuzzi el jacuzzi
jam *(food)* la mermelada
jammed *(stuck)* atascado(a)
January enero
Japan Japón
jar *(honey, jam, etc)* el tarro
jaundice la icericia
jaw la mandíbula
jazz el jazz
jealous celoso(a)
jeans los vaqueros
jelly *(dessert)* la gelatina
jellyfish la medusa
jet ski la moto acuática
jetty el embarcadero
Jewish judío(a)
jeweller's la joyería
jewellery las joyas
Jiffy bag® el sobre acolchado
job el empleo
to jog hacer footing
to join *(club, etc)* hacerse miembro de
joint *(body)* la articulación
to joke bromear
joke la broma
journalist el/la periodista

journey el viaje
judge el/la juez(a)
jug la jarra
juice el zumo
  apple juice el zumo de manzana
  orange juice el zumo de naranja
  tomato juice el zumo de tomate
  a carton of juice un brik de zumo
July julio
to jump saltar
jumper el jersey
jump leads *(for car)* los cables de arranque
junction *(road)* la bifurcación
June junio
jungle la jungla
just: *just two* sólo dos
  I've just arrived acabo de llegar

K

karaoke el karaoke
to keep *(to retain)* guardar
  keep the change quédese con la vuelta
kennel la caseta
kettle el hervidor (de agua)
key la llave
  card key (ie used in hotel) la llave tarjeta
keyring el llavero
kid *(young goat)* el cabrito
kidneys los riñones
to kill matar
kilo(gram) el kilo
kilogram el kilogramo
kilometre el kilómetro
kind *(person)* amable
king el rey
kiosk el quiosco
kiss el beso
to kiss besar
kitchen la cocina
kitchen paper el papel de cochina

kite la cometa
kitten el gatito
kiwi fruit el kiwi
knee la rodilla
knee highs las medias cortas
knickers las bragas
knife el cuchillo
to knit hacer punto
to knock *(on door)* llamar
to knock down *(car)* atropellar
to knock over *(vase, glass)* tirar
knot el nudo
to know *(have knowledge of)* saber
  (person, place) conocer
  I don't know no sé
to know how to saber
  to know how to swim saber
  nadar

L

label la etiqueta
lace *(fabric)* el encaje
laces *(for shoes)* los cordones
ladder la escalera de mano
ladies *(toilet)* los servicios de
  señoras
lady la señora
lager la cerveza
  bottled lager la cerveza de
  botella
  draught lager la cerveza de barril
lake el lago
lamb el cordero
lamp la lámpara
lamppost la farola
land el terreno
to land aterrizar
landlady la dueña (de la casa)
landlord el dueño (de la casa)
landslide el desprendimiento de
  tierras
lane el camino
  (of motorway) el carril
language el idioma

laptop el ordenador portátil
large grande
last último(a)
  the last bus el último autobús
  the last train el último tren
  last night anoche
  last week la semana pasada
  last year el año pasado
late tarde
  the train is late el tren viene
  con retraso
  sorry I'm late siento llegar tarde
later más tarde
to laugh reírse
launderette la lavandería
  automática
laundry service el servicio de
  lavandería
lavatory *(in house)* el wáter
  (in public place) los aseos ; los
  servicios
lavender lavanda
law la ley
lawyer el/la abogado(a)
laxative el laxante
layby la zona de descanso
lazy perezoso(a)
lead *(electric)* el cable
lead *(metal)* el plomo
lead-free sin plomo
leaf la hoja
leak *(of gas, liquid)* la fuga
  (in roof) la gotera
to leak: *it's leaking* *(radiator, etc)*
  está goteando
to learn aprender
lease *(rental)* el alquiler
leather la piel ; el cuero
to leave *(a place)* irse de
  (leave behind) dejar
  when does it leave? ¿a qué
  hora sale?
  when does the bus leave? ¿a
  qué hora sale el autobús?
  when does the train leave? ¿a
  qué hora sale el tren?

leek el puerro
left: *on/to the left* a la izquierda
left-handed *(person)* zurdo(a)
left-luggage *(office)* la consigna
leg la pierna
legal legal
leggings las mallas
leisure centre el polideportivo
lemon el limón
lemonade la gaseosa
lemon tea el té con limón
to lend prestar
length la longitud
lens *(photographic)* el objetivo
 (contact lens) la lentilla
Lent la Cuaresma
lentils las lentejas
lesbian lesbiana
less menos
lesson la clase
to let *(to allow)* permitir
 (to hire out) alquilar
letter la carta
 (of alphabet) la letra
letterbox el buzón
lettuce la lechuga
level crossing el paso a nivel
library la biblioteca
licence el permiso
 (driving) el carné de conducir
lid la tapa
lie *(untruth)* la mentira
lifebelt el salvavidas
lifeboat el bote salvavidas
lifeguard el/la socorrista
life insurance el seguro de vida
life jacket el chaleco salvavidas
life raft la balsa salvavidas
lift *(elevator)* el ascensor
 can you give me a lift? ¿me lleva?
lift pass *(on ski slopes)* el forfait
light *(not heavy)* ligero(a)
light la luz
 have you a light? ¿tiene fuego?

light bulb la bombilla
lighter el encendedor
lighthouse el faro
lightning el relámpago
to like gustar
 I like coffee me gusta el café
 I don't like... no me gusta...
 I'd like to... me gustaría...
 we'd like to... nos gustaría...
lilo la colchoneta hinchable
lime *(fruit)* la lima
line *(row, queue)* la fila
 (telephone) la línea
linen el lino
lingerie la lencería
lion el león
lips los labios
lip-reading la lectura de labios
lip salve el cacao para los labios
lipstick la barra de labios
liqueur el licor
list la lista
to listen to escuchar
litre el litro
litter *(rubbish)* la basura
little pequeño(a)
 a little un poco
to live vivir
 I live in Edinburgh vivo en Edimburgo
 he lives in a flat vive en un piso
liver el hígado
living room el cuarto de estar
lobster la langosta
local de la región ; del país
lock *(on door, box)* la cerradura
 the lock is broken la cerradura está rota
bike lock el candado de bicicleta
to lock cerrar con llave
locker *(luggage)* la consigna
log book *(car)* los papeles del coche
lollipop la piruleta ; el chupa-chups
London Londres
 in London en Londres

to London a Londres
long largo(a)
for a long time (por) mucho tiempo
long-sighted hipermétrope
to look after cuidar
to look at mirar
to look for buscar
loose suelto(a)
lorry el camión
to lose perder
lost perdido(a)
I've lost my wallet he perdido la cartera
I'm lost me he perdido
lost property office la oficina de objetos perdidos
lot: *a lot* mucho
lotion la loción
lottery la lotería
loud (sound, voice) fuerte (volume) alto(a)
lounge (in hotel) el salón (in house) el cuarto de estar
love el amor
to love (person) querer ; amar
I love swimming me encanta nadar
I love you te quiero ; te amo
lovely precioso(a)
low bajo(a)
low-fat bajo(a) en calorías
low tide la marea baja
lucky: *to be lucky* tener suerte
luggage el equipaje
luggage allowance el equipaje permitido
luggage rack el portaequipajes
luggage tag la etiqueta
luggage trolley el carrito
lump (swelling) el bulto (on head) el chichón
lunch el almuerzo ; la comida
lung el pulmón
luxury de lujo

machine la máquina
magazine la revista
maggot el gusano
magnet el imán
magnifying glass la lupa
magpie la urraca
maid (in hotel) la camarera
maiden name el apellido de soltera
mail el correo
by mail por correo
main principal
main course (of meal) el plato principal
Majorca Mallorca
make (brand) la marca
to make hacer *see* GRAMMAR
make-up el maquillaje
male masculino(a)
mallet el mazo
man el hombre
to manage (be in charge of) dirigir
manager el/la gerente
managing director el/la director(a) gerente
man-made fibre la fibra sintética
manual (gear change) manual
manure el estiércol
many muchos(as)
map (of region, country) el mapa (of town) el plano
marathon el maratón
marble el mármol
March marzo
margarine la margarina
marina el puerto deportivo
marinated en escabeche
marjoram la mejorana
mark (stain) la mancha
market el mercado
where is the market? ¿dónde está el mercado?

m

when is the market? ¿cuándo hay mercado?

marmalade la mermelada de naranja

married casado(a)
I'm married estoy casado(a)
are you married? ¿está casado(a)?

marrow el tuétano ; la médula

to marry casarse con

marsh la marisma

marzipan el mazapán

mascara el rímel®

mashed potato el puré de patatas

masher *(potato)* el pasapurés

mass *(in church)* la misa

mast el mástil

masterpiece la obra maestra

match *(game)* el partido

matches las cerillas

material *(cloth)* la tela

m

to matter importar
it doesn't matter no importa
what's the matter? ¿qué pasa?

mattress el colchón

May mayo

mayonnaise la mayonesa ; la mahonesa

meadow el prado

meal la comida

to mean querer decir
what does this mean? ¿qué quiere decir esto?

measles el sarampión

to measure medir

meat la carne
white meat la carne blanca
red meat la carne roja
I don't eat meat no como carne

mechanic el/la mecánico(a)

m

medical insurance el seguro médico

medicine la medicina

medieval medieval

Mediterranean el Mediterráneo

medium rare *(meat)* medio(a) hecho(a)

to meet *(by chance)* encontrarse con
(by arrangement) reunirse con
pleased to meet you encantado(a) de conocerle

meeting la reunión

melon el melón

to melt derretir

member *(of club, etc)* el/la socio(a)

men los hombres

to mend arreglar

meningitis la meningitis

menu la carta
set menu el menú del día

meringue el merengue

message el mensaje ; el recado

metal el metal

meter el contador

metre el metro

metro *(underground)* el metro

microwave oven el horno microondas

midday las doce del mediodía

middle el medio ; el centro

middle-aged de mediana edad

midge el mosquito enano

midnight la medianoche
at midnight a medianoche

migraine la jaqueca ; la migraña
I've a migraine tengo migraña

mile 5 miles = approx. 8 km

milk la leche
fresh milk la leche fresca
hot milk la leche caliente
long-life milk la leche de larga duración (UHT)
powdered milk la leche en polvo
semi-skimmed milk la leche semi-desnatada
skimmed milk la leche desnatada
soya milk la leche de soja
with milk con leche

milkshake el batido *[Lat. Am.* la malteada*]*

millimetre el milímetro
million el millón
mince *(meat)* la carne picada
mind: *do you mind if ...?* ¿le importa que...?
  I don't mind no me importa
mineral water el agua mineral
minimum el mínimo
minister *(political)* el/la ministro(a)
  (church) el/la pastor(a)
mink el visón
mint *(herb)* la menta
  (sweet) la pastilla de menta
minute el minuto
mirror el espejo
miscarriage el aborto no provocado
to miss *(train, etc)* perder
Miss la señorita
missing *(lost)* perdido(a)
  my son is missing se ha perdido mi hijo
mistake el error
misty: *it's misty* hay neblina
misunderstanding la equivocación
to mix mezclar
mixer *(food processor)* el robot
  (hand-held) la batidora
mobile phone el (teléfono) móvil
modem el módem
modern moderno(a)
moisturizer la leche hidratante
mole *(on skin)* el lunar
moment: *just a moment* un momento
monastery el monasterio
Monday lunes
money el dinero
  [Lat. Am. la plata]
  I've no money no tengo dinero
moneybelt la riñonera
money order el giro postal
monkey el mono
month el mes
  this month este mes
  last month el mes pasado

  next month el mes que viene
monthly mensualmente
monument el monumento
moon la luna
mooring el atracadero
mop la fregona
moped la moto ; la motocicleta
more más
  more than 3 más de tres
  more wine más vino
morning la mañana
  in the morning por la mañana
  this morning esta mañana
  tomorrow morning mañana por la mañana
mosque la mezquita
mosquito el mosquito
mosquito net la mosquitera
most: *most of* la mayor parte de
moth *(clothes)* la polilla
mother la madre
mother-in-law la suegra
motor el motor
motorbike la moto
motorboat la lancha motora
motorway la autopista
mountain la montaña
mountain bike la bicicleta de montaña
mountain rescue el rescate de montaña
mountaineering el montañismo
mouse *(animal, computer)* el ratón
mousse *(food)* la mousse
  (for hair) la espuma
moustache el bigote
mouth la boca
mouthwash el enjuague bucal
Mr el señor (Sr.)
Mrs la señora (Sra.)
Ms la señora (Sra.)
much mucho
  too much demasiado
mud el barro
mugging el atraco

m

mumps las paperas
muscle el músculo
museum el museo
mushroom el champiñón
music la música
musical musical
mussel el mejillón
must *(to have to)* deber
mustard la mostaza
mutton el cordero
my mi

N

nail *(fingernail)* la uña
  (metal) el clavo
nailbrush el cepillo de uñas
nail clippers el cortaúñas
nail file la lima de uñas
nail polish el esmalte de uñas
nail polish remover el quitaesmalte
nail scissors las tijeras de uñas
name el nombre
  my name is... me llamo...
  what's your name? ¿cómo se llama?
nanny la niñera
napkin la servilleta
nappies los pañales
narrow estrecho(a)
national nacional
national park el parque nacional
nationality la nacionalidad
nature la naturaleza
nature reserve la reserva natural
navy blue azul marino
near cerca de
  near to the bank cerca del banco
  is it near? ¿está cerca?
necessary necesario(a)
neck el cuello
necklace el collar
nectarine la nectarina
to need necesitar
  I need... necesito...

  we need... necesitamos...
  I need to go tengo que ir
needle la aguja
  a needle and thread una aguja e hilo
negative *(photo)* el negativo
neighbour el/la vecino(a)
nephew el sobrino
nest el nido
net la red
nettle la ortiga
never nunca
  I never drink wine nunca bebo vino
new nuevo(a)
news *(TV, radio, etc)* las noticias
newspaper el periódico
newsstand el kiosko de prensa
New Year el Año Nuevo
  happy New Year! ¡feliz Año Nuevo!
New Year's Eve la Nochevieja
New Zealand Nueva Zelanda
next próximo(a)
  next to al lado de
  next week la próxima semana
  the next stop la próxima parada
  the next train el próximo tren
nice *(person)* simpático(a)
  (place, holiday) bonito(a)
  [Lat. Am. lindo(a)*]*
niece la sobrina
night la noche
  at night por la noche
  last night anoche
  per night por noche
  tomorrow night mañana por la noche
  tonight esta noche
night club la discoteca
nightdress el camisón
no no
  no entry prohibida la entrada
  no smoking prohibido fumar
  (without) sin
  no sugar sin azúcar
  no ice sin hielo

nobody nadie
noise el ruido
  it's very noisy hay mucho ruido
non-alcoholic sin alcohol
none ninguno(a)
non-smoking no fumador
noodles los fideos
north el norte
Northern Ireland Irlanda del Norte
North Sea el Mar del Norte
nose la nariz
note *(banknote)* el billete
  (written) la nota
note pad el bloc
nothing nada
  nothing else nada más
notice *(sign)* el anuncio
  (warning) el aviso
notice board el tablón de anuncios
novel la novela
November noviembre
now ahora
nuclear nuclear
nudist beach la playa nudista
number el número
numberplate *(car)* la matrícula
nurse la/el enfermera(o)
nursery school la guardería infantil
nursery slope la pista para principiantes
nut *(for bolt)* la tuerca
nuts *(to eat)* los frutos secos
nutmeg la nuez moscada

O

oak el roble
oar el remo
oats la avena
to obtain obtener
obvious evidente
occasionally de vez en cuando
occupation *(work)* la profesión
ocean el océano

October octubre
octopus el pulpo
odd *(number)* impar
of de
  a glass of wine un vaso de vino
  made of ... hecho(a) de...
off *(light, etc)* apagado(a)
  (rotten) pasado(a)
office la oficina
often a menudo
  how often? ¿cada cuánto?
oil el aceite
oil filter el filtro de aceite
oil gauge el indicador del aceite
ointment la pomada
OK vale
old viejo(a)
  how old are you? ¿cuántos años tiene?
  I'm ... years old tengo ... años
old age pensioner el/la pensionista de la tercera edad
olive la aceituna ; la oliva
olive oil el aceite de oliva
olive tree el olivo
omelette la tortilla
on *(light, TV, engine)* encendido(a)
on sobre ; encima
  on the table sobre la mesa
  on time a la hora
once una vez
  at once en seguida
one uno(a)
one-way dirección única
onion la cebolla
only sólo
open abierto(a)
to open abrir
opera la ópera
operation *(surgical)* la operación
operator *(phone)* el/la telefonista
opposite (to) enfrente (de)
optician's la óptica

or o

tea **or** coffee té o café

orange *(fruit)* la naranja
(colour) color naranja

orange juice el zumo de naranja

orchard el huerto; la huerta

orchestra la orquesta

order: *out of order* averiado(a)

to order *(in restaurant)* pedir
can I order? ¿puedo pedir?

oregano el orégano

organic biológico(a)

to organize organizar

other: *the other one* el/la otro(a)
have you any others? ¿tiene
otros(as)?

ounce = approx. 30 g

our nuestro(a)

out *(light)* apagado(a)
he's (gone) out ha salido

out of order averiado(a)

outdoor *(pool, etc)* al aire libre

outside: *it's outside* está fuera

oven el horno

oven gloves la manopla de horno

ovenproof dish resistente al horno

over *(on top of)* (por) encima de

to be overbooked tener 'overbooking'

to overcharge cobrar demasiado

overcoat el abrigo

overdone *(food)* demasiado
hecho(a)

overdose la sobredosis

to overheat recalenatar

to overload sobrecargar

to overtake *(in car)* adelantar

to owe deber
I owe you... le debo...
you owe me... me debe...

owl el búho

owner el/la propietario(a)

oxygen el oxígeno

oyster la ostra

P

pacemaker el marcapasos

to pack *(luggage)* hacer las maletas

package el paquete

package tour el viaje organizado

packet el paquete

padded envelope el sobre
acolchado

paddling pool la piscina hinchable

padlock el candado

page la página

paid pagado(a)
I've paid he pagado

pain el dolor

painful doloroso(a)

painkiller el analgésico

to paint pintar

paintbrush el pincel

painting *(picture)* el cuadro

pair el par

palace el palacio

pale pálido(a)

pan *(saucepan)* la cacerola
(frying) la sartén

pancake el crep(e)

panniers *(for bike)* los maleteros

panties las bragas

pants *(men's underwear)* los calzoncillos

panty liner el salvaslips

paper el papel

paper napkins las servilletas de
papel

papoose *(for carrying baby)* la
mochila portabebés

paracetamol® el paracetamol®

paraffin la parafina

parcel el paquete

pardon? ¿cómo?
I beg your pardon! ¡perdón?

parents los padres

park el parque

to park aparcar

parking disk el tique de aparcamiento
parking meter el parquímetro
parking ticket (fine) la multa por aparcamiento indebido
parmesan el parmesano
parsley el perejil
parsnip la chirivía ; el nabo dulce
partner (business) el/la socio(a) (boy/girlfriend) el/la compañero(a)
party (group) el grupo (celebration) la fiesta (political) el partido
pass (mountain) el puerto (train) el abono (bus) el bonobús
passenger el/la pasajero(a)
passport el pasaporte
passport control el control de pasaportes
pasta la pasta
pastry (dough) la masa (cake) el pastel
pâté el paté
path el camino
patience (card game) el solitario
patient (in hospital) el/la paciente
pavement la acera
to pay pagar
  I'd like to pay quisiera pagar
  where do I pay ¿dónde se paga?
payment el pago
payphone el teléfono público
peace la paz
peach el melocotón
peak rate la tarifa máxima
peanut el cacahuete
peanut butter la mantequilla de cacahuete
pear la pera
pearls las perlas
peas los guisantes
pedal el pedal
pedestrian el peatón
pedestrian crossing el paso de peatones

to peel (fruit) pelar
peg (for clothes) la pinza (for tent) la clavija
pen el bolígrafo
penfriend el/la amigo(a) por correspondencia
pencil el lápiz
penicillin la penicilina
peninsula la península
penis el pene
penknife la navaja
pensioner el/la jubilado(a)
people la gente
pepper (spice) la pimienta (vegetable) el pimiento
per por
  per day por día ; al día
  per hour por hora
  per week a la semana
  per person por persona
  50 km per hour 50 km por hora
perch (fish) la perca
perfect perfecto(a)
performance: *next performance* la próxima función
perfume el perfume
perhaps quizás
period (menstruation) la regla
perm la permanente
permit el permiso
person la persona
  per person por persona
personal organizer la agenda
personal stereo el walkman®
pet el animal doméstico
petrol la gasolina
  4-star petrol la gasolina súper
  unleaded petrol la gasolina sin plomo
petrol cap el tapón del depósito
petrol pump el surtidor
petrol station la estación de servicio ; la gasolinera
petrol tank el depósito
pharmacy la farmacia
pheasant el faisán

p

127

p

phone el teléfono
  by phone por teléfono
to phone llamar por teléfono ;
  telefonear
phonebook la guía (telefónica)
phonebox la cabina (telefónica)
phone call la llamada (telefónica)
phonecard la tarjeta telefónica
photocopy la fotocopia
to photocopy fotocopiar
photograph la fotografía
  to take a photograph hacer una
  fotografía
phrase book la guía de
  conversación
piano el piano
pickled en vinagre
pickpocket el/la carterista
picnic el picnic
  to have a picnic ir de picnic
picnic area el merendero
picnic rug la mantita
picture *(painting)* el cuadro
  (photo) la foto
pie *(fruit)* la tarta
  (meat) el pastel de carne
  (and/or vegetable) la empanada
piece el trozo
pier el embarcadero ; el muelle
pig el cerdo
pill la píldora
  to be on the Pill tomar la píldora
pillow la almohada
pillowcase la funda
pilot el/la piloto
pin el alfiler
pine el pino
pineapple la piña
pine nut el piñón
pink rosa
pint = approx. 0.5 litre
pip la semilla ; la pepita
pipe *(smoker's)* la pipa
  (drain, etc) la tubería
pistachio el pistacho

pizza la pizza
place el lugar ; el sitio
plain *(yoghurt)* natural
plait la trenza
plan *(of town)* el plano
plane *(airplane)* el avión
plane tree el plátano
plant la planta
plaster *(sticking)* la tirita®
  (for broken limb) la escayola
plastic *(made of)* de plástico
plastic bag la bolsa de plástico
plate el plato
platform el andén
  which platform? ¿qué andén?
play *(theatre)* la obra
to play *(games)* jugar
playroom el cuarto de juegos
pleasant agradable
please por favor
pleased contento(a)
  pleased to meet you encanta-
  do(a) de conocerle
pliers los alicates
plug *(electrical)* el enchufe
  (for sink) el tapón
plum la ciruela
plumber el/la fontanero(a)
plunger *(for sink)* el desatascador
poached *(egg, fish)* escalfado(a)
pocket el bolsillo
point el punto
points *(in car)* los platinos
poison el veneno
poisonous venenoso(a)
police *(force)* la policía
policeman/woman el/la policía
police station la comisaría
polish *(for shoes)* el betún
  (for furniture) el limpiamuebles
polluted contaminado(a)
pony el poni
pony-trekking la excursión a
  caballo
poor pobre

128

pope el papa
poppy la amapola
pop socks las medias cortas
popular popular
pork el cerdo
port *(seaport)* el puerto
   (wine) el oporto
porter *(hotel)* el portero
   (at station) el mozo
portion la porción , la ración
portrait el retrato
Portugal Portugal
Portuguese portugués/portuguesa
   (language) el portugués
possible posible
post: by post por correo
to post echar
postbox el buzón
postcard la postal
postcode el código postal
poster el póster
postman/woman el/la cartero(a)
post office la oficina de correos
to postpone aplazar
pot *(for cooking)* la olla
potato la patata
   baked potato la patata asada
   boiled potatoes las patatas
   hervidas
   fried potatoes las patatas fritas
   mashed potatoes el puré de
   patatas
   roast potatoes las patatas
   asadas
   sautéed potatoes las patatas
   salteadas
potato masher el pasapurés
potato peeler el pelador
potato salad la ensalada de
   patatas
pothole el bache
pottery la cerámica
pound *(weight)* = approx. 0.5 kilo
   (money) la libra
to pour echar ; servir
powder: in powder form en polvo

powdered milk la leche en polvo
pram el cochecito (del bebé)
prawn la gamba
to pray rezar
to prefer preferir
pregnant embarazada
   I'm pregnant estoy embarazada
to prepare preparar
to prescribe prescribir
prescription la receta médica
present *(gift)* el regalo
pressure la presión
   blood pressure la presión arterial
pretty bonito(a)
price el precio
price list la lista de precios
priest el sacerdote
prince el príncipe
princess la princesa
print *(photo)* la copia
prison la cárcel
private privado(a)
prize el premio
probably probablemente
problem el problema
professor el/la catedrático(a)
programme *(TV, radio)* el programa
prohibited prohibido(a)
to promise prometer
to pronounce pronunciar
   how's it pronounced? ¿cómo se
   pronuncia?
Protestant protestante
prune la ciruela pasa
public público(a)
public holiday la fiesta
pudding el postre
to pull tirar
   I've pulled a muscle me ha
   dado un tirón en el músculo
pullover el jersey
pump *(bike, etc)* la bomba
   (petrol) el surtidor
pumpkin la calabaza
puncture el pinchazo

129

p

puppet la marioneta
puppet show el espectáculo de marionetas
puppy el cachorro
purple morado(a)
purpose: *on purpose* a propósito
purse el monedero
to push empujar
pushchair la silla de niño
to put *(place)* poner
pyjamas el pijama
Pyrenees los Pirineos

Q

quail la codorniz
quality la calidad
quantity la cantidad
quarantine la cuarentena
to quarrel discutir
quarter el cuarto
quay el muelle
queen la reina
question la pregunta
queue la cola
to queue hacer cola
quick rápido(a)
quickly de prisa
quiet *(place)* tranquilo(a)
quilt el edredón
quite bastante
 it's quite good es bastante bueno
 quite expensive bastante caro
quiz el concurso

R

rabbit el conejo
rabies la rabia
race *(sport)* la carrera
race course *(horses)* el hipódromo
rack *(luggage)* la rejilla
racket *(tennis, etc)* la raqueta
radiator *(car, heater)* el radiador

radio la radio
radishes los rábanos
rag el trapo
railway el ferrocarril
rain la lluvia
to rain: *it's raining* está lloviendo
rainbow el arco iris
raincoat el impermeable
raisin la pasa
rake el rastrillo
rape la violación
to rape violar
rare *(unique)* excepcional
 (steak) poco hecho(a)
rash *(skin)* el sarpullido
raspberries las frambuesas
rat la rata
rate *(price)* la tarifa
rate of exchange el tipo de cambio
raw crudo(a)
razor la maquinilla de afeitar
razor blades las hojas de afeitar
to read leer
ready listo(a)
 to get ready prepararse
real auténtico(a) ; verdadero(a)
rearview mirror el (espejo) retrovisor
receipt el recibo
receiver *(phone)* el auricular
recently recientemente
reception desk la recepción
receptionist el/la recepcionista
to recharge *(battery, etc)* recargar
recipe la receta
to recognize reconocer
to recommend recomendar
record *(music)* el disco
to recover *(from illness)* recuperarse
red rojo(a)
redcurrants las grosellas rojas
to reduce reducir
reduction el descuento
reel *(fishing)* el carrete

referee el/la árbitro
refill el recambio
refund el reembolso
to refuse negarse
region la región
to register *(at hotel)* registrarse
registered *(letter)* certificado(a)
registration form la hoja de registro
to reimburse reembolsar
relation *(family)* el/la pariente
to remain *(stay)* quedarse
to remember acordarse (de)
I don't remember no me acuerdo
remote control el mando a distancia
rent el alquiler
to rent alquilar
repair la reparación
to repair reparar
to repeat repetir
to reply contestar
report el informe
to request solicitar
to require necesitar
to rescue rescatar
reservation la reserva
to reserve reservar
reserved reservado(a)
resident el/la residente
resort el centro turístico
rest *(repose)* el descanso
(remainder) el resto de
to rest descansar
restaurant el restaurante
restaurant car el coche-restaurante
to retire jubilarse
retired jubilado(a)
to return *(to go back)* volver
(to give back something) devolver
return *(ticket)* de ida y vuelta
to reverse dar marcha atrás
reverse charge call la llamada a cobro revertido

reverse gear la marcha atrás
rheumatism el reumatismo
rhubarb el ruibarbo
ribbon la cinta
rice el arroz
rich *(person)* rico(a)
(food) pesado(a)
to ride a horse montar a caballo
right *(correct)* correcto(a)
to be right tener razón
right: on/to the right a la derecha
to ring *(bell, to phone)* llamar
ring el anillo
ring road la carretera de circunvalación
ripe maduro(a)
river el río
road la carretera
road sign la señal de tráfico
roadworks las obras
roast asado(a)
robin el petirrojo
roll *(bread)* el panecillo ; el bollo
rollerblades los patines en línea
rolling pin el rodillo
romance *(novel)* la novela romántica
Romanesque el románico
romantic romántico(a)
roof el tejado
roof-rack la baca
room *(in house, hotel)* la habitación
(space) sitio
double room la habitación doble
single room la habitación individual
room number el número de habitación
room service el servicio de habitaciones
root la raíz
rope la cuerda
rose la rosa
rosemary el romero

rosé wine el rosado
rotten *(fruit, etc)* podrido(a)
rough *(sea)* picado(a)
round *(shape)* redondo(a)
roundabout *(traffic)* la rotonda
row *(line)* la fila
to row *(boat)* remar
rowing *(sport)* el remo
rowing boat el bote de remos
royal real
rubber *(material)* la goma
   (eraser) la goma de borrar
rubber band la gomita
rubber gloves los guantes de
   goma
rubbish la basura
rubella la rubeola
rucksack la mochila
rudder el timón
rug la alfombra
ruins las ruinas
ruler *(for measuring)* la regla

rum el ron
to run correr
rush hour la hora punta
rusty oxidado(a)
rye el centeno

S

saccharin la sacarina
sad triste
saddle *(bike)* el sillín
   (horse) la silla de montar
safe seguro(a); sin peligro
   is it safe? ¿es seguro(a)?
safe *(for valuables)* la caja fuerte
safety belt el cinturón de seguridad
safety pin el imperdible
sage *(herb)* la salvia
to sail *(sport, leisure)* hacer vela
sailboard la tabla de windsurf
sailing *(sport)* la vela
sailing boat el barco de vela ; el

velero
saint el/la santo(a)
salad la ensalada
   green salad la ensalada verde
   mixed salad la ensalada mixta
   potato salad la ensalada de
   patatas
   tomato salad la ensalada de
   tomate
salad dressing el aliño
salami el salchichón ; el salami
sale(s) las rebajas
salesman/woman el/la vendedor(a)
sales rep el/la representante
salmon el salmón
   smoked salmon el salmón
   ahumado
salt la sal
salt water el agua salada
salty salado(a)
same mismo(a)
sample la muestra
sand la arena
sandals las sandalias
sandwich el bocadillo
   toasted sandwich el sandwich
sanitary towels las compresas
sardine la sardina
satellite dish la antena parabólica
satellite TV la televisión por
   satélite
Saturday sábado
sauce la salsa
   tomato sauce la salsa de tomate
saucepan la cacerola
saucer el platillo
sauna la sauna
sausage la salchicha
to save *(life)* salvar
   (money) ahorrar
saw la sierra
to say decir
scales *(weighing)* el peso
scallop la vieira
scampi las gambas

scarf *(woollen)* la bufanda
 (headscarf) el pañuelo
school la escuela
scissors las tijeras
score *(of match)* la puntuación
to score a goal marcar un gol
Scotland Escocia
Scottish escocés/escocesa
scouring pad las nanas®
screen *(computer, TV)* la pantalla
screenwash el limpiacristales
screw el tornillo
screwdriver el destornillador
 phillips screwdriver® el
 destornillador de estrella
scuba diving el submarinismo
sculpture *(object)* la escultura
sea el mar
seafood los mariscos
seagull la gaviota
seal la foca
seasick mareado(a)
seaside la playa
 at the seaside en la playa
season *(of year)* la estación
 in season del tiempo
season ticket el abono
seasoning el condimento
seat *(chair)* la silla
 (in bus, train) el asiento
seatbelt el cinturón de seguridad
seaweed las algas
second segundo(a)
second *(time)* el segundo
second class de segunda clase
second-hand de segunda mano
secretary el/la secretario(a)
security guard el/la guardia de
 seguridad
to see ver
seed la semilla
self-catering sin servicio de
 comidas
self-employed autónomo(a)
self-service el autoservicio

to sell vender
 do you sell...? ¿tiene...?
sell-by date la fecha de caducidad
Sellotape® el celo
semi-skimmed milk la leche
 semidesnatada
to send enviar
senior citizen el/la pensionista
separated *(couple)* separado(a)
separately: *to pay separately*
 pagar por separado
September septiembre
septic tank el pozo séptico
sequel *(film, etc)* la continuación
serious *(accident, etc)* grave
to serve servir
service *(in church)* la misa
 (in restaurant) el servicio
 is service included? ¿está
 incluido el servicio?
service charge el servicio
service station la estación de
 servicio
serviette la servilleta
set menu el menú del día
several varios(as)
to sew coser
sex el sexo
shade la sombra
to shake *(bottle)* agitar
shallow poco profundo(a)
shampoo el champú
shampoo and set lavar y marcar
shandy la cerveza con gaseosa
to share repartir
sharp *(razor, knife)* afilado(a)
to shave afeitarse
shaving cream la crema de afeitar
shawl el chal
she ella *see* **GRAMMAR**
sheep la oveja
sheet *(bed)* la sábana
shelf el estante
shell *(seashell)* la concha
 (egg, nut) la cáscara

S shellfish los mariscos
sheltered protegido(a)
shepherd el/la pastor(a)
sherry el jerez
to shine brillar
shingles *(illness)* el herpes zoster
ship el barco
shirt la camisa
shock absorber el amortiguador
shoe el zapato
shoelaces los cordones (de los zapatos)
shoe mender el zapatero
shoe polish el betún
shoe shop la zapatería
shop la tienda
shop assistant el/la dependiente(a)
shopping las compras
 to go shopping ir de compras
shopping centre el centro comercial
shore la orilla
S short corto(a)
short cut el atajo
shorts los pantalones cortos
short-sighted miope
shoulder el hombro
to shout gritar
show *(theatrical)* el espectáculo
to show enseñar
shower *(bath)* la ducha
 [Mexico la regadera]
 to take a shower ducharse
 (rain) el chubasco
shower cap el gorro de ducha
shower curtain la cortina de la ducha
shrimp el camarón
to shrink encogerse
shut *(closed)* cerrado(a)
S to shut cerrar
shutters los postigos
shy tímido(a)
sick *(ill)* enfermo(a)
 I feel sick (nauseous) tengo

ganas de vomitar
side el lado
side dish la guarnición
sidelight la luz de posición
sidewalk la acera
sieve *(for liquids)* el colador
 (for flour, etc) el tamiz
to sightsee hacer turismo
to sign firmar
signature la firma
signpost la señal
silk la seda
silver la plata
similar to parecido(a) a
since desde ; puesto que
 since 1974 desde 1974
 since you're not Spanish puesto que no es español(a)
to sing cantar
single *(unmarried)* soltero(a)
 (bed, room) individual
sink *(in kitchen)* el fregadero
sir señor
sister la hermana
sister-in-law la cuñada
to sit sentarse
size *(clothes)* la talla
 (shoes) el número
to skate patinar
skates los patines
skating rink la pista de patinaje
ski el esquí
 jet ski la moto acuática
to ski esquiar
ski boots las botas de esquí
ski instructor el/la monitor(a) de esquí
ski jacket la chaqueta de esquí
ski jump el salto de esquí
ski lift el telesquí
ski pants los pantalones de esquí
ski pass el forfait
ski pole/stick el bastón de esquí
ski run/piste la pista de esquí
ski suit el traje de esquí

skimmed milk la leche desnatada
skin la piel
skindiving el submarinismo
skirt la falda
sky el cielo
slang la jerga
sledge el trineo
to sleep dormir
  to sleep in quedarse dormido(a)
sleeper *(on train)* la litera
sleeping bag el saco de dormir
sleeping car el coche-cama
sleeping pill el somnífero
slice *(of bread)* la rebanada
  (of ham) la loncha
sliced bread el pan de molde
slide *(photograph)* la diapositiva
to slip resbalarse
slippers las zapatillas
slow lento(a)
to slow down reducir la velocidad
slowly despacio
small pequeño(a)
smell el olor
  a bad smell un mal olor
  a nice smell un buen olor
smile la sonrisa
to smile sonreír
to smoke fumar
  I don't smoke no fumo
smoke el humo
smoke alarm la alarma contra incendios
smoked ahumado(a)
smokers *(sign)* fumadores
snack el tentempié
  to have a snack tomar algo
snack bar la cafetería
snake la serpiente
snake bite la mordedura de serpiente
to sneeze estornudar
to snore roncar
snorkel el tubo de buceo

snow la nieve
to snow nevar
  it's snowing está nevando
snow board el snowboard
snow chains las cadenas (para la nieve)
snowman el muñeco de nieve
snow tyres los neumáticos anti-deslizantes
soap el jabón
soap powder el detergente
sober sobrio(a)
socket *(for plug)* el enchufe
socks los calcetines
soda water la soda
sofa el sofá
sofa bed el sofá-cama
soft blando
soft drink el refresco
software el software
soldier el soldado
sole *(fish)* el lenguado
  (of foot, shoe) la suela
soluble soluble
some algunos(as)
someone alguien
something algo
sometimes a veces
son el hijo
son-in-law el yerno
song la canción
soon pronto
  as soon as possible lo antes posible
sore throat el dolor de garganta
sorry: *sorry!* ¡perdón!
  I'm sorry! ¡lo siento!
sound el sonido
soup la sopa
sour amargo(a)
soured cream la nata agria
south el sur
souvenir el recuerdo
spa el balneario
spade la pala

135

S **Spain** España
Spanish español(a)
spanner la llave inglesa
spare parts los repuestos
spare tyre la rueda de repuesto
spare wheel la rueda de repuesto
sparkling espumoso(a)
   sparkling water el agua con gas
   sparkling wine el vino espumoso
spark plug la bujía
to speak hablar
specialist el/la especialista
speciality la especialidad
speed la velocidad
speed limit la velocidad máxima
   to exceed the speed limit
   exceder la velocidad máxima
speedboat la lancha motora
speedometer el velocímetro
spell: *how is it spelt?* ¿cómo se
   escribe?
to spend *(money)* gastar
S **spice** la especia
spicy picante
spider la araña
to spill derramar
spine la columna vertebral
spinach las espinacas
spirits el alcohol
splinter la astilla
spoke *(wheel)* el radio
sponge la esponja
spoon la cuchara
sport el deporte
sports shop la tienda de
   deportes
spot *(pimple)* la espinilla
sprain el esguince
spring *(season)* la primavera
spring onion la cebolleta
S **square** *(in town)* la plaza
squash *(game)* el squash
to squeeze apretar
   (lemon) exprimir
squid el calamar

stadium el estadio
stain la mancha
stained glass la vidriera
stairs las escaleras
stale *(bread)* duro(a)
stalls *(theatre)* las butacas (de
   patio)
stamp *(postage)* el sello
star la estrella
to start *(car)* poner en marcha
starter *(in meal)* entrante
   (in car) la puesta en marcha
station *(bus, rail, metro)* la estación
stationer's la papelería
statue la estatua
to stay *(remain)* quedarse ; estar
   I'm staying at hotel... estoy en
   el hotel…
steak el filete
   medium steak un filete en su
   punto
   well-done steak un filete muy
   hecho
   rare steak un filete poco hecho
to steal robar
steamed al vapor
steel el acero
steep: *is it steep?* ¿hay mucha
   subida?
steeple la aguja
steering wheel el volante
stepfather el padrastro
stepmother la madrastra
stereo el estéreo
   personal stereo el walkman®
sterling *(pounds)* las libras
   esterlinas
stew el estofado
steward *(on plane)* el auxiliar de
   vuelo
stewardess *(on plane)* la azafata
to stick *(with glue)* pegar
sticking plaster la tirita®
still *(not fizzy)* sin gas
sting la picadura
to sting picar

136

stitches *(surgical)* los puntos (de sutura)
stock cube la pastilla de caldo
stockings las medias
stomach el estómago
stomach upset el trastorno estomacal
stone la piedra
to stop parar
store *(shop)* la tienda
storey el piso
storm la tormenta
(at sea) el temporal
story la historia
straightaway inmediatamente
straight on todo recto
[Lat. Am. derecho]
strainer el colador
straw *(for drinking)* la pajita
strawberry la fresa
stream el arroyo
street la calle
street map el plano de la ciudad
stress el estrés
strike *(of workers)* la huelga
string la cuerda
striped a rayas
stroke *(medical)* el derrame cerebral
strong fuerte
stuck: *it's stuck* está atascado(a)
student el/la estudiante
stuffed relleno(a)
stung picado(a)
stupid tonto(a)
subscription la suscripción
subtitles los subtítulos
suddenly de repente
suede el ante
sugar el azúcar
  icing sugar el azúcar glasé
sugar-free sin azúcar
suit *(men's and women's)* el traje
suitcase la maleta
summer el verano

summer holidays las vacaciones de verano
sun el sol
to sunbathe tomar el sol
sunblock la protección solar total
sunburn la quemadura del sol
Sunday domingo
sunflower el girasol
sunflower oil el aceite de girasol
sunglasses las gafas de sol
sunny: *it's sunny* hace sol
sunrise la salida del sol
sunroof el techo solar
sunscreen el filtro solar
sunset la puesta de sol
sunshade la sombrilla
sunstroke la insolación
suntan el bronceado
suntan lotion el bronceador
supermarket el supermercado
supper la cena
supplement *(to pay)* el suplemento
to surf hacer surf
surfboard la tabla de surf
surgery *(operation)* la operación
surname el apellido
surprise la sorpresa
surrounded by rodeado(a) de
to swallow tragar
swan el cisne
to sweat sudar
sweater el jersey
sweatshirt la sudadera
sweet *(not savoury)* dulce
sweet *(dessert)* el dulce
sweetener el edulcorante ; la sacarina®
sweets los caramelos
to swell *(injury etc)* hincharse
to swim nadar
swimming pool la piscina
swimsuit el traje de baño
swing *(for children)* el columpio
Swiss suizo(a)

S

S

S

s

switch el interruptor
to switch off apagar
to switch on encender
Switzerland Suiza
swollen hinchado(a)
swordfish el pez espada
synagogue la sinagoga
syringe la jeringuilla

T

table la mesa
tablecloth el mantel
tablespoon la cuchara de servir
table tennis el ping-pong
tablet *(pill)* la pastilla
tail la cola
tailor's la sastrería
to take *(medicine, etc)* tomar
  how long does it take? ¿cuánto tiempo se tarda?
take-away *(food)* para llevar
to take off despegar
to take out *(of bag, etc)* sacar
talc los polvos de talco
to talk to hablar con
tall alto(a)
tame *(animal)* manso(a)
tampons los tampones
tangerine la mandarina
tank *(petrol)* el depósito
  (fish) la pecera
tap el grifo [*Lat. Am.* la llave]
tape *(video)* la cinta
tape measure el metro
tape recorder el magnetofón
tarragon el estragón
tart la tarta
tartar sauce la salsa tártara
taste el sabor
to taste probar
  can I taste it? ¿puedo probarlo?
tax el impuesto
taxi el taxi
taxi driver el/la taxista

taxi rank la parada de taxis
tea el té
  herbal tea la infusión (de hierbas)
  lemon tea el té con limón
  strong tea el té cargado
teabag la bolsita de té
teapot la tetera
teaspoon la cucharilla
tea towel el paño de cocina
to teach enseñar
teacher el/la profesor(a)
team el equipo
tear *(in material)* el rasgón
teat *(on baby's bottle)* la tetina
teeshirt la camiseta
teeth los dientes
telegram el telegrama
telephone el teléfono
  mobile phone el teléfono móvil
to telephone llamar por teléfono ; telefonear
telephone box la cabina telefónica
telephone call la llamada telefónica
telephone card la tarjeta telefónica
telephone directory la guía telefónica
telephone number el número de teléfono
television la televisión
telex el télex
to tell decir
temperature la temperatura
  to have a temperature tener fiebre
temple el templo
temporary provisional
tendon el tendón
tennis el tenis
tennis ball la pelota de tenis
tennis court la pista de tenis
tennis racket la raqueta de tenis
tent la tienda de campaña
tent peg la clavija

terminal *(airport)* la terminal
terrace la terraza
terracotta la terracota
terrorist el/la terrorista
testicles los testículos
than que
  more than you más que tú
  more than five más de cinco
to thank agradecer
thank you gracias
  thank you very much muchas
  gracias
that one eso ; aquello
theatre el teatro
theft el robo
their su
there *(over there)* allí
there is/there are hay
thermometer el termómetro
these estos/estas
  these ones éstos/éstas
they ellos/ellas see **GRAMMAR**
thief el ladrón/la ladrona
thigh el muslo
thin *(person)* delgado(a)
thing la cosa
  my things mis cosas
to think pensar
  (to be of opinion) creer
third tercero(a)
thirsty: *I'm thirsty* tengo sed
this one esto
thorn la espina
those ones esos ; aquellos
thousand mil
thread el hilo
thriller *(film)* la película de
  suspense
  (book) la novela de suspense
throat la garganta
throat lozenges las pastillas para
  la garganta
through por
thrush *(candida)* la candidiasis
thumb el pulgar

thunder el trueno
thunderstorm la tormenta
Thursday jueves
thyme el tomillo
ticket *(bus, train, etc)* el billete
  [Lat. Am. el boleto]
  (entrance fee) la entrada
  a single ticket un billete de ida
  a return ticket un billete de ida
  y vuelta
  a tourist ticket un billete turista
  a book of tickets un abono
ticket collector el/la revisor(a)
ticket office el despacho de
  billetes
tide *(sea)* la marea
  low tide la marea baja
  high tide la marea alta
tie la corbata
tights las medias
till *(cash desk)* la caja
till *(until)* hasta
  till 2 o'clock hasta las 2
time el tiempo
  (clock) la hora
  what time is it? ¿qué hora es?
timer *(on cooker)* el temporizador
timetable el horario
tin *(can)* la lata
tinfoil el papel albal®
tin-opener el abrelatas
tiny pequeño(a)
tip la propina
to tip dar propina
tipped *(cigarette)* con filtro
Tippex® el Típpex®
tired cansado(a)
tissues los pañuelos de papel
to a
  to London a Londres
  to the airport al aeropuerto
toast *(to eat)* el pan tostado; la
  tostada
  (raising glass) el brindis
tobacco el tabaco
tobacconist's el estanco

t

today hoy
toe el dedo del pie
together juntos(as)
toilet los aseos; los servicios
   toilet for disabled los servicios para minusválidos
toilet brush la escobilla del wáter
toilet paper el papel higiénico
toiletries los artículos de baño
token *(for bus)* el vale
toll *(motorway)* el peaje
tomato el tomate
tomato juice el zumo de tomate
tomato purée el puré de tomate
tomato sauce la salsa de tomate
tomato soup la sopa de tomate
tomorrow mañana
   tomorrow morning mañana por la mañana
   tomorrow afternoon mañana por la tarde
   tomorrow evening mañana por la tarde/noche

t

tongue la lengua
tonic water la tónica
tonight esta noche
tonsillitis la amigdalitis
too *(also)* también
   too big demasiado grande
   too small demasiado pequeño(a)
   too hot *(food)* demasiado caliente
   too noisy demasiado ruidoso(a)
tool el instrumento
toolkit el juego de herramientas
tooth el diente
toothache el dolor de muelas
toothbrush el cepillo de dientes
toothpaste la pasta de dientes
toothpick el palillo
top: *the top floor* el último piso
top *(of hill)* la cima
   on top of... sobre...

t

topless: *to go topless* hacer topless
torch *(flashlight)* la linterna
torn rasgado(a)

total *(amount)* el total
to touch tocar
tough *(meat)* duro(a)
tour *(trip)* la vuelta
   (of museum, etc) la visita
   guided tour la visita con guía
tour guide el/la guía turístico(a)
tourist el/la turista
tourist office la oficina de turismo
tourist route la ruta turística
tourist ticket el billete turístico
to tow remolcar
tow rope el cable de remolque
towel la toalla
tower la torre
town la ciudad
town centre el centro de la ciudad
town hall el ayuntamiento
town plan el plano de la ciudad
toy el juguete
toy shop la juguetería
tracksuit el chándal
traditional tradicional
traffic la circulación ; el tráfico
traffic jam el atasco
traffic lights el semáforo
trailer el remolque
train el tren
   by train en tren
   the next train el próximo tren
   the first train el primer tren
   the last train el último tren
trainers las zapatillas de deporte
tram el tranvía
tranquilliser el tranquilizante
to translate traducir
translation la traducción
to travel viajar
travel agent's la agencia de viajes
travel guide la guía de viajes
travel sickness el mareo
traveller's cheque el cheque de viaje
tray la bandeja
tree el árbol

trip la excursión
trolley *(luggage, shopping)* el carrito
trousers los pantalones
trout la trucha
truck el camión
true verdadero(a)
trunk *(luggage)* el baúl
trunks *(swimming)* el bañador
to try *(attempt)* probar
to try on *(clothes)* probarse
t-shirt la camiseta
Tuesday martes
tulip el tulipán
tuna el bonito ; el atún
tunnel el túnel
turkey el pavo
to turn girar
to turn around girar
to turn off apagar
  (tap) cerrar
to turn on *(light, etc)* encender
  (tap) abrir
turnip el nabo
turquoise *(colour)* turquesa
tweezers las pinzas
twice dos veces
twin-bedded room la habitación con dos camas
twins los/las mellizos(as)
  identical twins los/las gemelos(as)
to type escribir a máquina
typical típico(a)
tyre el neumático
tyre pressure la presión de los neumáticos

U

ugly feo(a)
ulcer *(mouth)* la llaga
  (stomach) la úlcera
umbrella el paraguas
  (sunshade) la sombrilla
uncle el tío

uncomfortable incómodo(a)
unconscious inconsciente
under debajo de
underground *(metro)* el metro
underpants los calzoncillos
underpass el paso subterráneo
to understand entender
  I don't understand no entiendo
  do you understand? ¿entiende?
underwear la ropa interior
underwater debajo del agua
to undress desvestirse
unemployed parado(a) ; desempleado(a)
to unfasten desabrocharse
United States Estados Unidos
university la universidad
unleaded petrol la gasolina sin plomo
to unpack *(suitcases)* deshacer las maletas
to unscrew destornillar
up: to get up levantarse
upside down al revés
upstairs arriba
urgent urgente
urine la orina
USA EE. UU.
to use usar
useful útil
usually por lo general
U-turn el cambio de sentido

V

vacancy *(in hotel)* la habitación libre
vaccination la vacuna
vacuum cleaner la aspiradora
vagina la vagina
valid válido(a)
valley el valle
valuable de valor
valuables los objetos de valor
value el valor

V

valve la válvula
van la furgoneta
vanilla vainilla
vase el florero
VAT el IVA
veal la ternera
vegan vegetaliano(a)
vegetables las verduras
vegetarian vegetariano(a)
 I'm vegetarian soy vegetariano(a)
vehicle el vehículo
vein la vena
Velcro® Velcro®
velvet el terciopelo
vending machine el distribuidor
 automático
venereal disease la enfermedad
 venérea
venison la carne de venado
ventilator el ventilador
very muy
vest la camiseta
vet el/la veterinario(a)
via por
to video *(from TV)* grabar (en
 vídeo)
video el vídeo
video camera la vídeocámara
video cassette la cinta de vídeo
video game el videojuego
video phone el videófono
video recorder el vídeo
view la vista
village el pueblo
vinaigrette la vinagreta
vinegar el vinagre
vineyard la viña ; el viñedo
violet *(flower)* la violeta
viper la víbora
virus el virus
visa el visado
to visit visitar
visiting hours *(hospital)* las horas
 de visita
visitor el/la visitante

vitamin la vitamina
vodka el vodka
voice la voz
volcano el volcán
volleyball el voleibol
voltage el voltaje
to vomit vomitar
voucher el vale

W

wage el sueldo
waist la cintura
waistcoat el chaleco
to wait for esperar
waiter/waitress el/la camarero(a)
waiting room la sala de espera
to wake up despertarse
Wales Gales
walk un paseo
 to go for a walk dar un paseo
to walk andar
walking boots las botas de
 montaña
walking stick el bastón
Walkman® el Walkman®
wall *(inside)* la pared
 (outside) el muro
wallet la cartera
walnut la nuez
to want querer *see* GRAMMAR
war la guerra
ward *(hospital)* la sala
wardrobe el ropero
warehouse el almacén
warm caliente
 it's warm (weather) hace calor
warning triangle el triángulo
 señalizador
to wash (oneself) lavar(se)
wash and blow dry lavado y
 secado a mano
washbasin el lavabo
washing machine la lavadora
washing powder el detergente

washing-up bowl el barreño de plástico

washing-up liquid el líquido lavavajillas

wasp la avispa

waste bin el cubo de la basura

to watch (look at) mirar

watch el reloj

watchstrap la correa de reloj

water el agua
cold water el agua fría
drinking water el agua potable
hot/cold water el agua caliente/fría
mineral water el agua mineral
sparkling water el agua con gas
still water el agua sin gas

watercress el berro

waterfall la cascada

water heater el calentador de agua

watermelon la sandía

waterproof impermeable
(watch) sumergible

to waterski el esquí acuático

waterwings los manguitos

waves (on sea) las olas

waxing (hair removal) la depilación (con cera)

way (manner) la manera
(route) el camino

way in (entrance) la entrada

way out (exit) la salida

we nosotros(as) *see* **GRAMMAR**

weak (coffee, tea) flojo(a)

to wear llevar

weather el tiempo

weather forecast el pronóstico del tiempo

web (spider) la telaraña
(internet) el Internet

website la página web

wedding la boda

wedding anniversary el aniversario de boda

wedding cake la tarta nupcial

wedding dress el vestido de boda

wedding present el regalo de boda

Wednesday miércoles

week la semana
last week la semana pasada
next week la semana que viene
per week por semana
this week esta semana

weekday el día laborable

weekend el fin de semana
next weekend el próximo fin de semana
this weekend este fin de semana

weekly semanalmente

to weigh pesar

weight el peso

welcome! ¡bienvenido(a)!

well (water) el pozo

well bien
he's not well no se encuentra bien

well done (steak) muy hecho(a)

wellington boots las botas de agua

Welsh galés/galesa
(language) el galés

west el oeste

wet mojado(a)
(weather) lluvioso(a)

wetsuit el traje de bucear

what? ¿qué?

wheel la rueda

wheelchair la silla de ruedas

wheel clamp el cepo

when? ¿cuándo?

where? ¿dónde?

which? ¿cuál?

while: *in a while* dentro de un rato

whipped cream la nata montada

whisky el whisky

white blanco(a)

who? ¿quién?

whole entero(a)

wholemeal bread el pan integral
whose? ¿de quién?
why? ¿por qué?
wide ancho(a)
widow la viuda
widower el viudo
width el ancho
wife la mujer
wig la peluca
wildlife la fauna y flora
to win ganar
wind el viento
windbreak el cortavientos
windmill el molino de viento
window la ventana
  (shop) el escaparate [*Lat. Am.* la vitrina]
  (in car, train) la ventanilla
windscreen el parabrisas
windscreen wipers los limpia-parabrisas
to windsurf hacer windsurf
windy: *it's windy* hace viento
wine el vino
  red wine el vino tinto
  white wine el vino blanco
  dry wine el vino seco
  rosé wine el vino rosado
  sparkling wine el vino espumoso
  house wine el vino de la casa
wine list la carta de vinos
wing mirror el retrovisor exterior
winter el invierno
with con
  with ice con hielo
  with milk con leche
  with sugar con azúcar
without sin
  without ice sin hielo
  without milk sin leche
  without sugar sin azúcar
wolf el lobo
woman la mujer
wood *(material)* la madera
  (forest) el bosque

wool la lana
word la palabra
work el trabajo
to work *(person)* trabajar
  (machine, car) funcionar
  it doesn't work no funciona
world el mundo
world wide mundial
worried preocupado(a)
worse peor
worth: *it's worth...* vale...
to wrap *(parcel)* envolver
wrapping paper el papel de envolver
wrinkles las arrugas
wrist la muñeca
to write escribir
  please write it down escríbalo, por favor
writing paper el papel de escribir
wrong: *what's wrong* ¿qué pasa?
wrought iron el hierro forjado

X

X-ray la radiografía

Y

yacht el yate
year el año
  this year este año
  next year el año que viene
  last year el año pasado
yellow amarillo(a)
Yellow Pages las Páginas amarillas
yes sí
yesterday ayer
yet: *not yet* todavía no
yoghurt el yogur
  plain yoghurt el yogur natural
yolk la yema

you *(polite sing.)* usted *see*
 GRAMMAR
  (polite plural) **ustedes**
  (sing. with friends) **tú**
  (plural with friends) **vosotros**
young joven
your *(polite)* **su** ; *(familiar)* tu
youth hostel el albergue juvenil

Z

zero el cero
zip la cremallera
zone la zona
zoo el zoo

A

a to ; at
  a la estación to the station
  a las 4 at 4 o'clock
  a 30 kilómetros 30 km away
abadejo *m* haddock
abadía *f* abbey
abajo below ; downstairs
abanico *m* fan *(hand-held)*
abeja *f* bee

ABIERTO open

abogado(a) *m/f* lawyer
abonado *m* season-ticket holder
abonar to pay ; to credit
abono *m* season ticket
aborto *m* abortion
  aborto no provocado miscarriage
abrebotellas *m* bottle opener
abrelatas *m* tin/can-opener
abrigo *m* coat

ABRIL April

abrir to open ; to turn on *(tap)*
abrocharse to fasten *(seatbelt, etc)*
absceso *m* abscess
abuela *f* grandmother
abuelo *m* grandfather
aburrido(a) boring
acá here
acabar to finish
acampar to camp
acceso *m* access
  acceso andenes to the platforms
  acceso prohibido no access
  acceso vías to the platforms
accidente *m* accident
aceite *m* oil
  aceite bronceador suntan oil
  aceite de oliva olive oil
aceituna *f* olive
  aceitunas aliñadas marinated olives
acelerador *m* accelerator

acento *m* accent
aceptar to accept
acera *f* pavement ; sidewalk
acero *m* steel
ácido *m* acid
acompañar to accompany
aconsejar to advise
acto *m* act
  en el acto while you wait *(repairs)*
actor *m* actor
actriz *f* actress
acuerdo *m* agreement
  ¡de acuerdo! OK ; alright
adaptador *m* adaptor *(electrical)*
adelantar to overtake *(in car)*
adelante forward
adicional extra ; additional
adiós goodbye
administración *f* management
admitir to accept ; to permit
  no se admiten... ...not permitted
adolescente *m/f* teenager

ADUANA customs

adulto(a) *m/f* adult
advertir to warn
aerodeslizador *m* hovercraft
aerolínea *f* airline
aeropuerto *m* airport
aerosol *m* aerosol
afeitarse to shave
afiche *m* poster ; sign *(Lat. Am.)*
aficionado(a) *m/f* fan *(cinema, jazz, etc)*
afilado(a) sharp *(razor, knife)*
agarrar to take ; to catch *(bus, etc Lat. Am.)*
agencia *f* agency
  agencia de seguros insurance company
  agencia de viajes travel agency
agenda *f* diary ; personal organizer
agente *m/f* agent
  agente de policía policeman/woman

a agitar to shake *(bottle)*

AGOSTO August

agotado(a) sold out ; out of stock
agradable pleasant
agradecer to thank
agridulce sweet and sour
agua *f* water
  agua caliente/fría hot/cold water
  agua destilada distilled water
  agua dulce fresh water
  agua mineral mineral water
  agua potable drinking water
  agua salada salt water
agudo(a) sharp ; pointed
águila *f* eagle
aguja *f* needle ; hand *(on watch)*
  aguja hipodérmica hypodermic
  needle
agujero *m* hole
ahogarse to drown
ahora now
a ahorrar to save *(money)*
ahumado(a) smoked
aire *m* air
  al aire libre open-air ; outdoor
aire acondicionado *m* air-
  conditioning
ajo *m* garlic
ala *f* wing
alargador *m* extension *(electrical)*
alarma *f* alarm
albahaca *f* basil
albarán *m* delivery note
albaricoque *m* apricot
albergue *m* hostel
  albergue juvenil youth hostel
alcanzar to reach ; to get
alcohol *m* alcohol ; spirits
alcohólico(a) alcoholic
a alemán/alemana German
Alemania *f* Germany
alergia *f* allergy
  alergia al polen hay fever
alérgico(a) a allergic to

aletas *fpl* flippers
alfarería *f* pottery
alfiler pin
alfombra *f* carpet *(rug)*
alforjas *fpl* panniers *(for bike)*
algas *fpl* seaweed
algo something
algodón *m* cotton
  algodón hidrófilo cotton wool
alguien someone
alguno(a) any
algunos(as) some ; a few
alicates *mpl* pliers
alimentación *f* grocer's ; food
alimento *m* food
aliño *m* dressing *(for food)*
allí there *(over there)*
almacén *m* store ; warehouse
  grandes almacenes department
  stores
almendra *f* almond
almohada *f* pillow
almuerzo *m* lunch
alojamiento *m* accommodation
  alojamiento y desayuno bed
  and breakfast
alpargatas *fpl* espadrilles
alquilar to rent ; to hire

SE ALQUILA for hire

alquiler *m* rent ; rental
  alquiler de coches car hire
alrededor about ; around
alto(a) high ; tall
  alta tensión high voltage
altura *f* altitude ; height
alubia *f* bean
  alubias blancas butter beans
  alubias pintas red kidney
  beans
amable pleasant ; kind
amapola *f* poppy
amargo(a) bitter ; sour
amarillo(a) yellow ; amber *(traffic
  light)*

148

ambientador m air freshener

ambos(as) both

ambulancia f ambulance

ambulatorio m health centre

América del Norte f America

amigo(a) friend
  amigo(a) por correspondencia penfriend

amor m love

amortiguador m shock absorber

ampolla f blister

analgésico m painkiller

análisis m analysis
  análisis de sangre blood test

ananá(s) m pineapple (Lat. Am.)

ancho m width

ancho(a) wide

anchoa f anchovy (salted)

anchura f width

ancla f anchor

andaluz(a) Andalusian

andar to walk

ANDÉN platform

añejo(a) mature ; vintage

anestesia f anaesthetic
  anestesia local local anaesthetic
  anestesia general general anaesthetic

anfiteatro m circle (theatre)

angina de pecho f angina

anillo m ring

animal m animal
  animal doméstico pet

anís m liqueur ; aniseed

aniversario m anniversary
  aniversario de boda wedding anniversary

año m year
  Año Nuevo New Year's Day

ante m suede

anteojos mpl binoculars ; spectacles (Lat. Am.)

antes (de) before

antiácido m antacid

antibiótico m antibiotic

anticonceptivo m contraceptive

anticongelante m antifreeze

anticuario m antique shop

antigüedades fpl antiques

antiguo(a) old ; ancient

antihistamínico m antihistamine

antiséptico m antiseptic

anual annual

anular to cancel

anunciar to announce ; to advertise

anuncio m advertisement ; notice

anzuelo m hook (fishing)

apagado(a) off (light, etc)

apagar to switch off ; to turn off

aparato m appliance

aparcamiento m car park

aparcar to park

apartadero m lay-by (Lat. Am.)

apartado de Correos m PO Box

apartamento m flat (apartment)

apellido m surname
  apellido de soltera maiden name

apendicitis f appendicitis

aperitivo m apéritif ; appetizer

apertura f opening

apio m celery

aplazar to postpone

apostar por to bet on

aprender to learn

apretar to squeeze

apto(a) suitable

aquí here
  aquí tiene... here is...

araña f spider

árbitro m referee

árbol m tree

arco iris m rainbow

ardor de estómago m heartburn

arena f sand

armario m wardrobe ; cupboard

arquitecto(a) m/f architect

arquitectura f architecture

arrancar to start

arreglar to fix ; to mend
arriba upstairs ; above
  hacia arriba upward(s)
arroyo *m* stream
arroz *m* rice
arruga *f* wrinkle
arte *f* art
artesanía *f* crafts
artesano(a) *m/f* craftsman/woman
articulación *f* joint *(body)*
artículo *m* article
  artículos de ocasión bargains
  artículos de tocador toiletries
artista *m/f* artist
artritis arthritis
asado(a) roast
asar a la parrilla to barbecue

ASCENSOR lift

asegurado(a) insured
asegurar to insure

ASEOS toilets

asiento *m* seat
  asiento para niños child safety
  seat
asistencia *f* help ; assistance
  asistencia técnica repairs
asma *m* asthma
aspirador *m* vacuum cleaner
aspirina *f* aspirin
astilla *f* splinter
atacar to attack
atajo *m* short cut
ataque *m* fit *(seizure)*
  ataque epiléptico epileptic fit
atascado(a) jammed *(stuck)*
atasco *m* hold-up *(traffic jam)*
aterrizar to land
ático *m* attic
atracadero *m* mooring

atraco *m* mugging
atrás behind
atropellar to knock down *(car)*
ATS *m/f* nurse

atún *m* tuna fish
audífono *m* hearing aid
aumentar to increase
auricular *m* receiver *(phone)*
auriculares *mpl* headphones
auténtico(a) genuine ; real
auto-stop *m* hitch-hiking
autobús *m* bus
autocar *m* coach *(bus)*
automático(a) automatic
autónomo(a) self-employed
autopista *f* motorway
autor(a) *m/f* author
autoservicio *m* self-service
auxiliar de vuelo *m/f* air steward/
stewardess
Av./Avda. abbrev. for **avenida**
avalancha *f* avalanche
ave *f* bird
  aves de corral poultry
avellana *f* hazelnut
avena *f* oats
avenida *f* avenue
avería *f* breakdown *(car)*
averiado(a) out of order ; broken
down
avión *m* airplane ; aeroplane
aviso *m* notice ; warning
avispa *f* wasp
ayer yesterday
ayudar to help
ayuntamiento *m* town hall
azafata *f* air hostess
azafrán *m* saffron
azúcar *m* sugar
  azúcar glasé icing sugar
azul blue
  azul claro light blue
  azul marino dark/navy blue

DIA AZUL cheap day for train
travel

ZONA AZUL controlled parking
area

B

babero m baby's bib
baca f roof rack
bahía f bay *(along coast)*
bailar to dance
baile m dance
bajar to go down(stairs) ; to drop *(temperature)*
bajarse (del) to get off *(bus, etc)*
bajo(a) low ; short ; soft *(sound)*
  bajo en calorías low-fat
  más bajo lower
balcón m balcony
balneario m spa
balón m ball
baloncesto m basketball
balsa salvavidas f life raft
bañador m swimming costume/trunks
banana f banana
bañarse to go swimming ; to bathe ; to have a bath
banca f banking ; bank
banco m bank ; bench
banda f band *(musical)*
bandeja f tray
bandera f flag
bañista m/f bather
baño m bath ; bathroom
  con baño with bath
bar bar
barato(a) cheap
barba f beard
barbacoa f barbecue
barbería f barber's
barbilla f chin
barca f small boat
barco m ship ; boat
  barco de vela sailing boat
barra f bar ; counter ; bread stick
  barra de labios lipstick
  barra de pan French bread
barreño de plástico m washing-up bowl

barrera f barrier ; crash barrier
barrio m district ; suburb
  barrio chino red light district
barro m mud
bastante enough ; quite
bastón m walking stick
  bastón de esquí ski pole/stick
basura f rubbish ; litter *(rubbish)*
bata f dressing gown
bate m bat *(baseball, cricket)*
batería f battery *(in car)*
batido m milkshake
batidora f blender *(hand-held)*
baúl m trunk *(luggage)*
bautizo m christening
bebé m baby
beber to drink
bebida f drink
  bebida sin alcohol soft drink
beicon m bacon
béisbol m baseball
berenjena f aubergine
berro m watercress
berza f cabbage
besar to kiss
beso m kiss
betún m shoe polish
biberón m baby's bottle
biblioteca f library
bicicleta f bicycle
  bicicleta de montaña mountain bike
bien well
bienvenido(a) welcome
bifurcación f fork *(in road)*
bigote m moustache
billete m ticket
  billete de ida y vuelta return ticket
  billete turístico tourist ticket
billetera f wallet
bistec m steak
bisutería f costume jewellery
blanco(a) white
  dejar en blanco leave blank *(on form)*

b

blando(a) soft
bloc m note pad
blusa f blouse
boca f mouth
bocadillo m sandwich *(made with French bread)*
boda f wedding
bodega f wine cellar ; restaurant
boite f night club
boleto m ticket *(Lat. Am.)*
bolígrafo m biro ; pen
bollo m roll ; bun
bolsa f bag ; stock exchange
bolsillo m pocket
bolsita de té f teabag
bolso m handbag
bomba f pump *(bike, etc)* ; bomb
bombero m fireman
bomberos mpl fire brigade
bombilla f light bulb
bombona de gas f gas cylinder
bombonería f confectioner's
bombones mpl chocolates
bonito(a) pretty ; nice-looking
bono m voucher
bono-bús m bus pass
borracho(a) drunk
bosque m forest ; wood
bota f boot
bote m boat ; tin ; can
  bote neumático rubber dinghy
  bote salvadidas lifeboat
botella f bottle
botines mpl boots *(short)*
botón m button
bragas fpl knickers
brazo m arm
brécol m broccoli
bricolaje m do-it-yourself *(shop)*
brillar to shine
brindis m toast *(raising glass)*
británico(a) British
broma f joke
bromear to joke
bronceado m suntan

bronceado(a) sun-tanned
bronceador m suntan lotion
broncearse to tan
bronquitis f bronchitis
brújula f compass
bucear to dive
bueno(a) good ; fine
  ¡buenos días! good morning!
  ¡buenas tardes! good afternoon/evening!
  ¡buenas noches! good evening/night!
bufanda f scarf *(woollen)*
bufet m buffet
búho m owl
bujía f spark plug
bulto m lump *(swelling)*
buñuelo m fritter ; doughnut
bunyi m bungee jumping
buscar to look for
butacas fpl stalls *(theatre)*
butano m Calor gas®
butifarra f Catalan sausage
buzón m postbox ; letterbox

C

CABALLEROS gents

caballo m horse
  montar a caballo to go riding
cabello m hair
cabeza f head
cabina f cabin
  cabina telefónica phone box
cable m wire ; cable
  cables de arranque jump leads
  cable de remolque tow rope
cabra f goat
cacahuete m peanut
cacao m cocoa
  cacao para los labios lip salve
cacerola f saucepan
cachemira f cashmere
cada every ; each

152

cada día daily *(each day)*
cada uno (c/u) each (one)
cadera f hip
caducado(a) out-of-date
caducar to expire *(ticket, passport)*
caer(se) to fall
café m café ; coffee
  café cortado espresso with dash of milk
  corto de café milky coffee
  café descafeinado decaff coffee
  café exprés espresso coffee
  café en grano coffee beans
  café con hielo iced coffee
  café con leche white coffee
  café instantáneo instant coffee
  café molido ground coffee
  café solo black coffee
cafetera f cafetière
cafetería f snack bar ; café

CAJA cashdesk

  caja de ahorros savings bank
  caja de cambios gearbox
  caja de fusibles fuse box
  caja fuerte safe
cajero(a) m/f teller ; cashier
  cajero automático cash dispenser ; auto-teller
cajón m drawer
calabacín m courgette
calabaza f pumpkin
calamares mpl squid
calambres mpl cramps
calcetines mpl socks
calculadora f calculator
caldereta f stew *(fish, lamb)*
caldo m stock ; consommé
calefacción f heating
calendario m calendar
calentador m heater
  calentador de agua water heater
calentar to heat up *(milk, food)*
calentura f cold sore
calidad f quality

CALIENTE hot

calle f street ; fairway *(golf)*
  callejón sin salida cul-de-sac
calmante m painkiller
calvo(a) bald
calzada f roadway
  calzada deteriorada uneven road surface
calzado m footwear
  calzados shoe shop
calzoncillos mpl underpants
cama f bed
  dos camas twin beds
  cama individual single bed
  cama de matrimonio double bed
cámara f camera ; inner tube
camarera f waitress ; chambermaid
camarero m barman ; waiter
camarote m cabin
cambiar to change ; to exchange
  cambiarse to get changed

CAMBIO bureau de change

caminar to walk
camino m path ; road ; route
  camino particular private road
camión m lorry ; bus *(Lat. Am.)*
camisa f shirt
camisería f shirt shop
camiseta f t shirt ; vest
camisón m nightdress
campana f bell *(church)*
camping m campsite
campo m countryside ; field ; pitch
  campo de fútbol football pitch
  campo de golf golf course
caña f cane ; rod
  caña de cerveza glass of beer
  caña de pescar fishing rod
Canadá m Canada
canadiense Canadian
Canal de la Mancha m English Channel
canasto m basket

C

cancelación *f* cancellation
cancelar to cancel
cáncer *m* cancer
cancha de tenis *f* tennis court
canción *f* song
candado *m* padlock
  candado de bicicleta bike lock
candela *f* candle
candidiasis *f* thrush
canela *f* cinnamon
canguro *m* kangaroo
canguro *m/f* babysitter
canoa *f* canoe
cansado(a) tired
cantante *m/f* singer
cantar to sing
cantidad *f* quantity
capilla *f* chapel
capital *f* capital *(city)*
capitán *m* captain
capó *m* bonnet ; hood *(of car)*
capucha *f* hood *(jacket)*

C

cara *f* face
caramelo *m* sweet ; caramel
caravana *f* caravan
carbón *m* coal
  carbón vegetal charcoal
carburador *m* carburettor
carburante *m* fuel
cárcel *f* prison
cargar to load
  cargar en cuenta to charge to
  account
cargo *m* charge
  a cargo del cliente at the
  customer's expense
Caribe *m* Caribbean
carnaval *m* carnival
carne *f* meat
  carne asada roast meat
  carne picada mince *(meat)*
carné de conducir driving licence
carné de identidad *m* identity card
carnicería *f* butcher's
caro(a) dear ; expensive

carpintería *f* carpenter's shop
carrera *f* career ; race *(sport)*
carrete *m* film *(for camera)* ;
  fishing reel
carretera *f* road ; highway
  carretera de circunvalación ring
  road
carril *m* lane *(on road)*
carrito *m* trolley
carro *m* car *(Lat. Am.)*
carta *f* letter ; playing card ; menu
  carta aérea air mail letter
  carta certificada registered letter
  carta verde green card
  carta de vinos wine list
cartel *m* poster
cartelera *f* entertainments guide
cartera *f* wallet ; briefcase
carterista *m/f* pickpocket
cartero(a) *m/f* postman/woman
cartón cardboard
casa *f* home ; house ; household
  casa de socorro first-aid post
casado(a) married
casarse con to marry
cascada *f* waterfall
cáscara *f* shell *(egg, nut)*
casco *m* helmet
casero(a) home-made
  comida casera home cooking
caseta *f* beach hut ; kennel
casete *m* cassette
casi almost
caso: en caso de in case of
caspa *f* dandruff
castaña *f* chestnut
castañuelas *fpl* castanets
castellano(a) Spanish ; Castilian
castillo *m* castle
catalán(lana) Catalonian
catálogo *m* catalogue
catedral *f* cathedral
católico(a) Catholic
causa *f* cause
  a causa de because of

causar to cause
cava m sparkling white wine
caza f hunting ; game
cazar to hun
cebo m bait *(for fishing)*
cebolla f onion
ceder: to give way
  ceda el paso give way
celeste light blue
celo m Sellotape®
celoso(a) jealous
cementerio m cemetery
cena f dinner *(eve meal)* , supper
cenar to have dinner *(eve meal)*
cenicero m ashtray
centímetro m centimetre
centralita f switchboard
centro m centre
Centroamérica f Central America
cepillo m brush
  cepillo de dientes toothbrush
  cepillo de uñas nailbrush
  cepillo del pelo hairbrush
cera f wax
cerámica f ceramics ; pottery
cerca (de) near ; close to
cercanías fpl outskirts ; proximity
  de cercanías suburban
cerdo m pig ; pork ; boar
cereza f cherry
cerillas fpl matches
cero zero

CERRADO closed

cerrado por reforma closed for
repairs
cerradura f lock
cerrar con llave to lock
cerro m hill
certificado m certificate
  certificado de seguros insurance
  certificate
certificado(a) registered
certificar to register
cervecería f pub

cerveza f beer ; lager
cesta f basket
cestería f basketwork *(shop)*
chalé m villa
chaleco m waistcoat
  chaleco salvavidas life jacket
champán m champagne
champiñón m mushroom
champú m shampoo
chancletas fpl flip flops
chaqueta f jacket
charcutería f delicatessen
cheque m cheque
  cheque de viaje traveller's
  cheque
chica f girl
chichón m lump *(on head)*
chico m boy
chico(a) small
chile m chilli
chimenea f fireplace ; chimney
chiringuito m bar
chocar to crash *(car)*
chocolate m chocolate ; hot
  chocolate
  chocolate puro plain chocolate
chocolatería f café serving hot
  chocolate
chófer m chauffeur ; driver
chorizo m type of salami ; hard
  pork sausage
chubasco m shower *(rain)*
chuleta f cutlet ; chop
chupete m dummy *(for baby)*
churrería f fritter shop or stand
churro m fritter
ciclista m/f cyclist
ciego(a) blind
cielo m sky ; heaven
cien hundred
CIF tax number *(for business)*
cifra f number ; figure
cigarra f cicada
cigarrillo m cigarette
cigarro m cigar ; cigarette

cima f top ; peak
cine m cinema
cinta f tape ; ribbon
  cinta de vídeo video cassette
  cinta virgen blank tape
cintura f waist
cinturón m belt
  cinturón de seguridad safety belt
circulación f traffic
circular to drive ; to circulate
  circule por la derecha keep right *(road sign)*
ciruela f plum
ciruela pasa f prune
cirujano(a) m/f surgeon
cisterna f cistern
cistitis f cystitis
cita f appointment
ciudad f city ; town
ciudadano(a) m/f citizen
clarete m light red wine
claro(a) light *(colour)* ; clear
clase f class ; type ; lesson
  clase preferente club/business class
  clase turista economy class
clavícula f collar bone
clavija f tent peg
clavo m nail *(metal)* ; clove *(spice)*
cliente m/f customer ; client
climatizado(a) air-conditioned
clínica f clinic ; private hospital
club nocturno m night club
cobrador m conductor *(bus)*
cobrar to charge ; to cash
  cobrar demasiado to overcharge
cobro m payment
cocer to cook ; to boil
coche m car ; coach (on train)
coche-cama m sleeping car
coche-comedor m dining car
coche-restaurante m restaurant car
cochecito (del bebé) m pram
cocido m thick stew

cocido(a) cooked ; boiled
cocina f kitchen ; cooker ; cuisine
cocinar to cook
coco m coconut
código m code
  código de barras barcode
  código postal post-code
codo m elbow
coger to catch ; to get ; to pick up (phone)
cola f glue ; queue ; tail
colador m strainer ; colander
colchón m mattress
colega m/f colleague
colegio m school
colgar to hang up (phone)
coliflor f cauliflower
colina f hill
colisionar to crash
collar m necklace
color m colour
columna vertebral f spine
columpio m swing *(for children)*
comedor m dining room
comenzar to begin
comer to eat
comercio m trade ; business
comestibles mpl groceries
comida f food ; meal
  se sirven comidas meals served
  comidas caseras home cooking
comisaría f police station
¿cómo? how? ; pardon?
como as ; like ; since
cómodo(a) comfortable
compañero/a m/f colleague ; boyfriend/girlfriend
compañía f company
compartimiento m compartment

COMPLETO no vacancies/full

comportarse to behave
compositor(a) m/f composer
compra f purchase
  compras shopping

comprar to buy
comprender to understand
compresas fpl sanitary towels
comprobar to check
con with
concha f sea-shell
concierto m concert
concurrido(a) busy ; crowded
concurso m competition ; quiz
condón m condom
conducir to drive
conductor(a) m/f driver
conectar to connect ; to plug in
conejo m rabbit
conferencia f conference
confirmación f confirmation
confirmar to confirm
confitería f cake shop
confitura f jam
congelado(a) frozen
congelador m freezer
conjunto m group (music)
conmoción cerebral f concussion
conocer to know ; to be
  acquainted with
conseguir to obtain
conserje m caretaker
conservar to keep
conservas fpl tinned foods

CONSIGNA left-luggage

construir to build
consulado m consulate
consultorio m doctor's surgery
consumición f consumption ;
  drink
consumir to eat ; to use
  consumir antes de... best
  before...
contacto m contact ; ignition (car)
contador m meter
contagioso(a) infectious
contaminado(a) polluted
contener to hold (to contain)
contenido m contents

contento(a) pleased
contestador automático m
  answerphone
contestar to answer ; to reply
continuación f sequel (film, etc)
continuar to continue
contra against
contrato m contract
control m inspection ; check
convento m convent ; monastery
copa f glass ; goblet
  copa de helado mixed ice
  cream
  tomar una copa to have a drink
copla f copy ; print (photo)
copiar to copy
corazón m heart
corbata f tie
corcho m cork
cordero m lamb ; mutton
cordillera f mountain range
coro m choir
correa f strap ; belt
  correa de reloj watchstrap
correcto(a) right (correct)
correo m mail
  correo electrónico e-mail
Correos m post office
correr to run
corrida de toros f bullfight
corriente f power ; current
  (electric, water) ; draught (of air)
cortacircuitos m circuit breaker
cortado m espresso with dash of
  milk
cortado(a) blocked (road)
cortar to cut
corte m cut
cortina f curtain
corto(a) short
cosa f thing
cosecha f harvest ; vintage (wine)
coser to sew
costa f coast
costar to cost

C

C

C

157

c **costero(a)** coastal

costumbre f custom *(tradition)*

coto m reserve
  coto de caza hunting by licence
  coto de pesca fishing by licence

crédito m credit
  a crédito on credit

creer to think ; to believe ; to be of opinion

crema f cream *(lotion)*
  crema de afeitar shaving cream
  crema bronceadora suntan lotion

cremallera f zip

crisis nerviosa f nervous breakdown

cruce m junction ; crossroads

crucero m cruise

crucigrama m crossword puzzle

crudo(a) raw

cruzar to cross

c/u (cada uno) each (one)

c **cuaderno** m exercise book

cuadro m picture ; painting
  a cuadros checked *(pattern)*

cuajada f curd

¿cuál? which?

¿cuándo? when?

¿cuánto? how much?

¿cuántos? how many?

cuarentena f quarantine

Cuaresma f Lent

cuarto m room ; quarter
  cuarto de baño bathroom
  cuarto de estar living room

cubierto m cover charge *(in restaurant)* ; menu

cubierto(a) covered ; indoor

cubiertos mpl cutlery

cubo m bucket ; pail ; bin

cubrir to cover

c **cucaracha** f cockroach

cuchara f spoon ; tablespoon

cucharilla f teaspoon

cuchillo m knife

cuenta f bill ; account *(at bank,etc)*

cuerda f string ; rope

cuero m leather

cuerpo m body

cuidado m care
  ¡cuidado! look out!
  ten cuidado be careful!

cuidadoso(a) careful

cultivar to grow ; to farm

cumpleaños m birthday
  ¡feliz cumpleaños! happy birthday!

cuna f cradle ; cot

cuñado(a) m/f brother/sister-in-law

curita f elastoplast *(Lat. Am.)*

curva f bend ; curve
  curvas peligrosas dangerous bends

D

dados mpl dice

daltónico(a) colour-blind

DAMAS ladies

daños mpl damage

dar to give
  dar de comer to feed
  dar marcha atrás to reverse
  dar propina to tip *(waiter, etc)*
  dar un paseo to go for a walk

dátil m date *(fruit)*

datos mpl data ; information

DCHA. abbrev. for **derecha**

de of ; from

de acuerdo all right *(agreed)*

debajo (de) under ; underneath

deber to owe ; to have to

debido(a) due

decir to tell ; to say

declarar to declare

dedo m finger
  dedo del pie toe

defecto m fault ; defect

degustación f tasting *(wine, etc)*

dejar to let ; to leave
  dejar libre la salida keep clear
delante de in front of
delegación f police station (Lat. Am.)
delgado(a) thin ; slim
delicioso(a) delicious
delito m crime
demasiado too much
  demasiado hecho(a) overdone
demora f delay
denominación de origen guarantee of quality of wine
dentadura postiza f dentures
dentífrico m toothpaste
dentista m/f dentist
dentro (de) inside
departamento m compartment ; department
dependiente m/f sales assistant
deporte m sport
depósito de gasolina m petrol tank
derecha f right(-hand side)
  a la derecha on/to the right
derecho m right ; law
  derechos de aduana customs duty
derecho(a) right ; straight
derramar to spill
derretir to melt
desabrochar to unfasten
desafilado(a) blunt (knife, blade
desaparecer to disappear
desarrollar to develop
desatascador m plunger (for sink)
desayuno m breakfast
descafeinado(a) decaffeinated
descansar to rest
descanso m rest ; interval
descarga electrica f electric shock
descargado(a) flat (battery)
descolgar to take down ; to pick up (phone)
descongelar to defrost ; to de-ice

describir to describe
descubrir to discover
descuento m discount ; reduction
desde since ; from
desear to want
desembarcadero m quay
desempleado(a) unemployed
desenchufado(a) off ; disconnected
deseo m wish ; desire
desfile m parade
deshacer to undo ; to unpack
desinfectante m disinfectant
desmaquillador m make-up remover
desmayado(a) fainted
desnatado(a) skimmed
desodorante m deodorant
despacho m office
despacio slowly ; quietly
despegar to take-off
despertador m alarm (clock)
despertarse to wake up
después after ; afterward(s)
desteñir: no destiñe colourfast
destino m destination
destornillador m screwdriver
  destornillador de estrella phillips screwdriver
destornillar to unscrew
desvestirse to get undressed
desvío m detour ; diversion
detalle m detail ; nice gesture
  al detalle retail (commercial)
detener to arrest
detergente m detergent ; washing powder
detrás (de) behind
deuda f debt
devolver to give/put back
día m day
  todo el día all day
  día festivo public holiday
  día laborable working day ; weekday
diabético(a) m/f diabetic

d

diamante m diamond
diario(a) daily
diarrea f diarrhoea
dibujo m drawing
diccionario m dictionary

DICIEMBRE December

diente m tooth
dieta f diet
difícil difficult
¡diga! hello *(on phone)*
dinero m money
  dinero en efectivo cash
Dios m God
diplomático(a) m/f diplomat
dirección f direction ; address
  dirección de correo electrónico
  e-mail address
  dirección particular home
  address
  dirección prohibida no entry
  dirección única one-way
directo(a) direct *(train, etc)*
director(a) m/f director ; manager
dirigir to manage *(be in charge of)*
disco m record ; disk
  disco de estacionamiento
  parking disk
  disco duro hard disk
discoteca f disco ; nightclub
discrecional optional
discutir to quarrel
diseño m design ; drawing
disquete m computer disk *(floppy)*
disponible available
distancia f distance
distinto(a) different
distribuidor automático m vending machine
distrito m district
DIU m coil *(IUD)*
diversión f fun
divertido(a) funny *(amusing)*
divertirse to enjoy oneself
divisa f foreign currency

divorciado(a) divorced
doblado(a) dubbed *(film)* ; folded
doblar to fold
doble double
docena f dozen
documentos mpl documents
dólar m dollar
dolor m ache ; pain
  dolor de cabeza headache
  dolor de garganta sore throat
  dolor de muelas toothache
  dolor de oídos earache
doloroso(a) painful
domicilio m home address

DOMINGO Sunday

dominó m dominoes
¿dónde? where?
dormir to sleep
dormitorio m bedroom
dorso m back
  véase al dorso please turn over
dosis f dose ; dosage
droga f drug
ducha f shower
ducharse to take a shower
dueño(a) m/f owner
dulce sweet
  el agua dulce fresh water
dulce m dessert
durante during
duro(a) hard ; tough

E

echar to post ; to pour ; to throw
ecológico(a) organic
edad f age *(of person)*
  edad mínima age limit
edificio m building
edredón m duvet ; quilt
edulcorante m sweetener
EE. UU. USA
efecto m effect
  efectos personales belongings

eje m axle (car)
ejemplar m copy (of book)
el the
él he see **GRAMMAR**
electricidad f electricity
electricista m/f electrician
eléctrico(a) electric(al)
elegir to choose
elevador m lift ; elevator (Lat. Am.)
ella she see **GRAMMAR**
ello it
ellos(as) they see **GRAMMAR**
embajada f embassy
embalse m reservoir
embarazada pregnant
embarcadero m jetty ; pier
embarcarse to board
embarque m boarding
embrague m clutch (in car)
emisión f broadcasting (radio, TV)
emitido por issued by
emocionante exciting
empachado(a) upset (stomach)
empezar to begin
empleo m employment ; use
empresa f firm ; company
empujar to push

EMPUJE push

en in ; into ; on
encaje m lace (fabric)
encantado(a) pleased to meet you!
encargado(a) m/f person in charge
encargar to order in advance
encendedor m cigarette lighter
encender to switch on ; to light
　encender las luces switch on
　headlights
encendido(a) on (light, TV, engine)
enchufar to plug in
enchufe m plug ; point ; socket
encima de onto ; on top of
encontrar to find
encontrarse con to meet (by
　chance)

ENERO January

enfadado(a) angry
enfermedad f disease
enfermera f nurse
enfermería f infirmary ; first-aid
　post
enfermo(a) ill
enfrente (de) opposite
¡enhorabuena! congratulations!
enjuagar to rinse
enjuague bucal m mouthwash
enlace m connection (train, etc)
ensalada f salad
enseñar to show ; to teach
entender to understand
entero(a) whole
entierro m funeral

ENTRADA entrance/admission

　entrada libre admission free
　entrada por delante enter at
　the front
entrar to go in ; to get in ;
　to enter
entre among ; between
entreacto m interval
entregar to deliver
entremeses mpl hors d'œuvres
entrevista f interview
envase m container ; packaging
enviar to send
envío m shipment
envolver to wrap
epiléptico(a) epileptic
equipaje m luggage ; baggage
　equipaje de mano hand-luggage
equipo m team ; equipment
equitación f horseriding
equivocación f mistake ;
　misunderstanding
error m mistake
es he/she/it is
escala f stopover

e

e

e

escalar to climb *(mountains)*
escalera f stairs ; ladder
  escalera de incendios fire escape
  escalera de mano ladder
  escalera mecánica escalator
escaleras stairs
escalón m step *(stair)*
escapar to escape
escaparate m shop window
escenario m theatre stage
escoba f broom *(brush)*
escocés/escocesa Scottish
Escocia f Scotland
escoger to choose
esconder to hide
escribir to write
escrito: por escrito in writing
escuchar to listen to
escuela f school
escultura f sculpture *(object)*
escurrir to wring
esguince m sprain
esmalte m varnish
esos/esas those
espacio m space
espalda f back *(of body)*
España f Spain
español(a) Spanish
espantoso(a) awful
esparadrapo m sticking plaster
especia f spice
especialidad f speciality
especialista m/f specialist
espectáculo m entertainment ; show
  espectáculo de marionetas puppet show
espejo m mirror
  espejo retrovisor rear-view mirror
esperar to wait (for) ; to hope
  espere su turno please wait your turn
espina f fish bone ; thorn
  espina dorsal spine
espinacas fpl spinach

espinilla f spot *(pimple)*
esponja f sponge
esposa f wife
esposo m husband
espuma f foam ; mousse *(for hair)*
  espuma de afeitar shaving foam
espumoso(a) frothy ; sparkling
esq. abbrev. for **esquina**
esquí m skiing ; ski
  esquí acuático water-skiing
  esquí de fondo cross-country skiing
esquiar to ski
esquina f street corner
está you/he/she/it is
estación f railway station ; season
  estación de autobuses bus/coach station
  estación de servicio petrol/service station
estacionamiento m parking space
estacionar to park
estadio m stadium
Estados Unidos mpl United States
estanco m tobacconist's
estante m shelf
estar to be *see* **GRAMMAR**
estatua f statue
este m east
este/ésta this one
estéreo m stereo
estómago m stomach
estornudar to sneeze
estos(as) these
estragón tarragon
estrecho(a) narrow
estrella f star
estreñimiento m constipation
estreno m première ; new release
estropeado(a) out of order
estudiante m/f student
etiqueta f label ; ticket ; tag
  de etiqueta formal dress
Euro Euro

Eurocheque *m* Eurocheque
Europa *f* Europe
evidente obvious
evitar to avoid
examen *m* examination
excelente excellent
excepcional rare *(unique)*
excepto except
exceso *m* excess
excursión *f* tour ; excursion
excusado *m* toilet *(Lat. Am.)*
éxito *m* success
expedido(a) issued
experto(a) expert
explicar to explain
exportación *f* export
exportar to export
exposición *f* exhibition
expreso *m* express train
exprimir to squeeze
extintor *m* fire extinguisher
extranjero(a) *m/f* foreigner
  en el extranjero abroad

F

f.c. abbrev. for **ferrocarril**
fabada *f* pork and bean stew
fábrica *f* factory
fácil easy
factura *f* receipt ; bill ; account
  factura detallada itemized bill
facturación *f* check-in
falda *f* skirt
falso(a) fake
falta *f* foul *(football)*
faltriquera *f* moneybelt
familia *f* family
famoso(a) famous
farmacia *f* chemist's ; pharmacy
  farmacia de guardia duty
  chemist
faro *m* headlamp ; lighthouse
  faro antiniebla fog-lamp
farola *f* lamppost

faros *mpl* headlights
favor *m* favour
  por favor please
favorito(a) favourite
fax *m* fax

FEBRERO February

FECHA date

  fecha de adquisición date of
  purchase
  fecha de caducidad expiry date
  fecha de expedición date of
  issue
  fecha de nacimiento date of
  birth
feliz happy
  ¡feliz año nuevo! happy New
  Year!
femenino(a) feminine
feo(a) ugly
feria *f* trade fair ; funfair
ferrocarril (f.c.) *m* railway
festivos *mpl* public holidays
fiambre *m* cold meat
fianza *f* bail bond ; deposit
fibra sintética *f* man-made fibre
ficha *f* token ; counter
fichero *m* file *(computer)*
fiebre *f* fever
fiesta *f* party ; public holiday
fila *f* row ; line *(row, queue)*
filete *m* fillet ; steak
filial *f* branch
filtro *m* filter
  filtro de aceite oil filter
  filtro solar sunscreen
fin *m* end
  fin de semana weekend
finalizar to end ; to finish
finca *f* farm ; property
fino *m* light, dry, very pale sherry
firma *f* signature
firmar to sign

  FIRME AQUÍ sign here

f

flete m freight
flojo(a) weak (coffee, tea)
flor f flower
florero m vase
floristería f florist's shop
foca f seal
foco m spotlight ; headlamp
folleto m leaflet ; brochure
fonda f inn ; small restaurant
fondo m bottom (of pool, etc)
fontanero m plumber
forfait m lift pass (skiing)
formulario m form
fósforo m match
foto f picture ; photo
fotocopia f photocopy
fotocopiar to photocopy
fotografía f photograph
fotógrafo(a) m/f photographer
fractura f fracture
frágil fragile ; handle with care
francés(esa) French
Francia f France
frecuente frequent
fregadero m sink (in kitchen)
fregona f mop (for floor)
freír to fry
frenar to brake
freno m brake
frente a opposite
frente m forehead
fresa f strawberry
fresco(a) fresh ; crisp ; cool
frigorífico m fridge

FRÍO cold

frito(a) fried
frontera f border ; frontier
frotar to rub
fruta f fruit
  fruta del tiempo fruit in season
frutería f fruit shop
frutos secos m nuts (to eat)
fuego m fire

fuente f fountain
fuera outdoors ; out
fuerte strong ; loud
fuga f leak (of gas, liquid)

FUMADORES smokers

fumar to smoke
  prohibido fumar no smoking
función f show
funcionar to work (machine, car)

NO FUNCIONA out of order

funcionario(a) m/f civil servant
funda f crown (for tooth) ; pillow-case ; case
  funda de gafas glasses case
funda nórdica f duvet cover
fusible m fuse
fútbol football
futbolista m/f football player

G

gafas fpl glasses
  gafas de sol sunglasses
galería f gallery
  galería de arte art gallery
galés/galesa Welsh
gallego(a) Galician
galletas fpl biscuits
ganar to earn ; to win (sports, etc)
garaje m garage
garantía f guarantee
garganta f throat
gas m gas
  gas butano Calor gas®
  con gas fizzy
  sin gas non-fizzy ; still
gasa f gauze ; nappy
gaseosa f lemonade
gasoil m diesel fuel
gasóleo m diesel oil
gasolina f petrol
  gasolina sin plomo unleaded petrol
  gasolina súper 4-star petrol

gasolinera f petrol station
gastado(a) flat *(tyre)*
gastar to spend *(money)*
gastos mpl expenses
gastritis f gastritis
gato m cat ; jack *(for car)*
gaviota f seagull
gemelo(a) m/f identical twin
gendarme m/f policeman/woman *(Lat. Am.)*
gendarmería f police (Lat. Am.)
género m type ; material
generoso(a) generous
gente f people
gerente m/f manager/manageress
ginebra f gin
girar to turn around
globo m balloon
glorieta f roundabout
golfo de Vizcaya m Bay of Biscay
goma f rubber ; eraser
gomita f rubber band
gordo(a) fat
gorra f cap *(hat)*
gotera f hole
Gótico(a) Gothic
grabar en vídeo to video *(from TV)*
gracias thank you
grada f tier
gramo m gram(me)
Gran Bretaña f Great Britain
grande large ; big ; tall
grandes almacenes mpl department store
granja f farm
granjero(a) m/f farmer
grasiento(a) greasy
gratinado(a) au gratin ; grilled
gratinar to grill
gratis free *(costing nothing)*
grave serious *(accident, etc)*
grifo m tap
gripe f flu
gris grey

gritar to shout
grosella negra f blackcurrant
grosella roja f redcurrant
grúa f crane ; breakdown van
grueso(a) thick *(not thin)*
grupo m group ; band *(rock)*
  grupo sanguíneo blood group
guacamole m avocado dip
guantes mpl gloves
  guantes de goma rubber gloves
guapo(a) handsome ; attractive
guardacostas m/f coastguard
guardar to put away ; to keep
guardarropa m cloakroom
guardería f nursery
guardería infantil f nursery school
guardia f guard
  Guardia Civil Civil Guard
  Guardia Nacional National Guard
  de guardia on duty
guarnición f garnish
guerra f war
guía m/f courier ; guide
  Guía del ocio What's on
  guía telefónica phone directory
guiar to guide
guindilla f chilli pepper
guiso m stew ; casserole
guitarra f guitar
gusano m maggot ; worm
gustar to like ; to enjoy

H

haba f broad bean
habano m Havana cigar
habitación f room
  habitación doble double room
  habitación individual single room
hablar (con) to speak/talk (to)
  se habla inglés English spoken
hacer to do ; to make *see* **GRAMMAR**
  hacer auto-stop to hitchhike
  hacer cola to queue
  hacer daño to hurt ; to damage

165

h

hacer 'footing' to jog
hacer las maletas to pack (case)
hacer punto to knit
hacer surf to surf
hacer topless to go topless
hacer transbordo de to change (bus/train)
hacer turismo to sightsee
hacia toward(s)
hacia adelante forwards
hacia atrás backwards
hacienda f farm ; ranch (Lat. Am.)
hamburguesa f hamburger
harina f flour
hasta until ; till
hay there is/there are
hecho(a) finished ; done
hecho a mano handmade
hecho(a) de... made of ...
helada f frost
heladería f ice-cream parlour
helado m ice cream
helicóptero m helicopter
hemorragia f haemorrhage
hemorroides fpl haemorrhoids
hepatitis f hepatitis
herida f wound ; injury
herido(a) injured
herir to hurt
hermana f sister
hermano m brother
hermoso(a) beautiful
hernia f hernia
herramienta f tool
hervido(a) boiled
hervidor (de agua) kettle
hervir to boil
hidrofoil m hydrofoil
hidropedal m pedal boat/pedalo
hielo m ice
con hielo with ice
hierba f grass ; herb
hierbabuena f mint
hierro m iron (metal)
hierro forjado wrought iron
hígado m liver

higo m fig
higos chumbos prickly pears
hija f daughter
hijo m son
hilo m thread
hincha m/f fan (football, etc)
hinchado(a) swollen
hipermercado m hypermarket
hipermétrope long sighted
hípica f showjumping
hipódromo m racecourse (horses)
histórico(a) historic
hogar m home ; household
hoja de registro f registration form
hojas de afeitar fpl razor blades
hola hello ; hi!
hombre m man
hombro m shoulder
hora f hour ; appointment
hora punta rush hour
horas de visita visiting hours
horario m timetable
horchata de chufa f refreshing tigernut drink
hormiga f ant
horno m oven
horno microondas microwave
al horno baked ; roasted
horquilla f hairgrip
hospital m hospital
hostal m small hotel ; hostel
hotel m hotel
hoy today
huelga f strike (of workers)
hueso m bone
huésped(a) m/f guest
huevo m egg
huevos de corral free-range eggs
huevo de pascua Easter egg
huevos duros hard-boiled eggs
huevos escalfados poached eggs
huevos al plato baked eggs
huevos revueltos scrambled eggs
humo m smoke

I

ida f outward journey
  de ida y vuelta return (ticket)
idioma m language
iglesia f church
igual equal
imán m magnet
impar odd (number)
imperdible m safety pin
impermeable m raincoat ; water-proof
importante important
importar to matter
importe total m total (amount)
imprescindible essential
impreso m form
  impreso de solicitud application form
impresos mpl printed matter
impuesto m tax
incendio m fire
incluido(a) included
incómodo(a) uncomfortable
inconsciente unconscious
indicaciones fpl directions
índice m index
indigestión f indigestion
individual individual ; single
infarto m heart attack
infección f infection
inferior inferior ; lower
inflamación f inflammation

INFORMACIÓN information

informe m report (medical, police)
infracción f offence
  infracción de tráfico traffic offence
ingeniero(a) m\f engineer
Inglaterra f England ; Britain
inglés/inglesa English
ingredientes mpl ingredients

inhalador m inhaler (for medication)
inmediatamente immediately
inmunización f immunisation
inquilino(a) m/f tenant
insecto m insect
insolación f sunstroke
instituto m institute ; secondary school
instrucciones fpl directions ; instructions
instructor(a) m/f instructor
instrumento m tool
insulina f insulin
interesante interesting
interior inside
intermitente m indicator (in car)
internacional international
internet m internet
intérprete m/f interpreter
interruptor m switch
intoxicación por alimentos f food poisoning
introducir to introduce ; to insert
  introduzca monedas insert coins
inundación f flood
invierno m winter
invitación f invitation
invitado(a) m/f guest
invitar to invite
inyección f injection
ir to go
  ir a buscar to fetch
  ir de compras to go shopping
  ir en bicicleta to cycle
  irse a casa to go home
  irse de... to leave (a place)
Irlanda f Ireland
Irlanda del Norte Northern Ireland
irlandés/irlandesa Irish
isla f island
Italia f Italy
italiano(a) Italian
itinerario m route ; schedule

i

IVA *m* VAT
IZQ. / IZQDA. abbrev. for izquierda
izquierda *f* left
izquierdo(a) left

J

jabón *m* soap
jamás never
jamón *m* ham
  jamón serrano cured ham
  jamón York boiled ham
Japón *m* Japan
jaqueca *f* migraine
jardín *m* garden
jarra *f* jug ; mug ; carafe
jefe(a) *m/f* chief ; head ; boss
jerez *m* sherry
jerga *f* slang
jeringuilla *f* syringe
joven young
joya *f* jewel
  joyas jewellery
joyería *f* jeweller's
jubilado(a) *m/f* retired person
jubilarse to retire
judías *fpl* beans
judío(a) Jew
juego *m* game

j

JUEVES Thursday

juez(a) *m/f* judge
jugador(a) *m/f* player
jugar to play ; to gamble

JULIO July

jugo *m* juice
juguete *m* toy
juguetería *f* toy shop

JUNIO June

junto(a) together
  junto a next to
juventud *f* youth

j

K

kilo *m* kilo(gram)
kilometraje *m* = mileage
  kilometraje ilimitado unlimited mileage
kilómetro *m* kilometre
kiosko de prensa *m* newsstand
kiwi *m* kiwi fruit

L

la the ; her ; it
labio *m* lip
laborable working *(day)*

  LABORABLES weekdays

laca *f* hair spray
lado *m* side
  al lado de beside
ladrar to bark
ladrillo *m* brick
ladrón(a) *m/f* thief
lago *m* lake
lámpara *f* lamp
lana *f* wool
lancha *f* launch
  lancha motora motor launch
lápiz *m* pencil
  lápiz de ojos eyeliner
largo(a) long
  largo recorrido long-distance *(train, etc)*
lata *f* can *(container)* ; tin
latón *m* brass
lavable washable
lavabo *m* lavatory ; washbasin
lavado de coches *m* car wash
lavado(a) washed
  lavado en seco dry-cleaning
  lavado y marcado shampoo and set
lavadora *f* washing machine
lavanda *f* lavender

lavandería f laundry
  lavandería automática
  launderette
lavavajillas m dishwasher
lavar to wash
  lavarse to wash oneself
laxante m laxative
leche f milk
  leche de soja soya milk
  leche de vaca cow's milk
  leche desnatada skimmed milk
  leche entera full cream milk
  leche hidratante moisturizer
  leche semidesnatada semi-
  skimmed milk
lechuga f lettuce
lector de CD m CD player
lectura de labios f lip-reading
leer to read
legumbres fpl pulses
lejía f bleach
lejos far
lencería f lingerie ; linen ; draper's
lengua f language ; tongue
lente f lens
  lentes de contacto contact lenses
lentejas fpl lentils
lentillas fpl contact lenses
lento(a) slow
león m lion
lesbiana f lesbian
letra f letter (of alphabet)
levantar to lift
levantarse to get up ; to rise
ley f law
libra f pound (currency, weight)
  libra esterlina pound sterling (£)

LIBRE free/vacant

  libre de impuestos tax-free
  dejen el paso libre keep clear
librería f bookshop
libro m book
licencia f permit ; licence
licenciarse to graduate
licor m liqueur

licores mpl spirits
lidia f bullfight
ligero(a) light (not heavy)
lima f file (for nails) ; lime
límite m limit ; boundary
  límite de velocidad speed limit
limón m lemon
limonada f lemonade
limpiar to clean
limpieza en seco f dry-cleaning
limpio(a) clean
lindo(a) nice (Lat. Am.)
línea f line
lino m linen
linterna f torch ; flashlight

LIQUIDACIÓN sales

líquido m liquid
  líquido de frenos brake fluid
liso(a) plain ; smooth
lista f list
  lista de correos poste restante
  lista de precios price list
  listo(a) para comer ready-cooked
listo(a) ready
litera f berth ; couchette ; sleeper
litoral m coast
litro m litre
llaga f ulcer (mouth)
llamada f call
  llamada a cobro revertido
  reverse charge call
llamar to call ; to ring ; to knock
  (on door)
llano(a) flat
llanta f tyre
llave f key ; tap ; spanner
  llave de contacto ignition key
  llaves del coche car keys
  llave inglesa spanner
  llave tarjeta card key
llavero m keyring
Lleg. abbrev. for **llegadas**
llegada f arrival
  llegadas (Lleg.) arrivals
llegar to arrive ; to come

llenar to fill ; to fill in
lleno(a) full (up)
 lleno, por favor fill it up, please
llevar to bring ; to wear ; to carry
 para llevar to take away
llorar to cry (weep)
lluvia f rain
lobo m wolf
local m premises ; bar
localidad f place
localidades fpl tickets (theatre)
loción f lotion
loncha f slice (ham, etc)
Londres m London
longitud f length
lotería f lottery
luces fpl lights
luchar to fight
lugar m place
 lugar de nacimiento place of birth
 lugar de expedición issued in
 lugar fresco cool place
lujo m luxury
luna f moon
 luna de miel honeymoon

LUNES Monday

lupa f magnifying glass
luz f light
 luz de freno brake light
 luz de posición sidelight

M

macedonia f fruit salad
madera f wood
madrastra f stepmother
madre f mother
maduro(a) ripe ; mature
magnetofón m tape recorder
maíz m maize ; corn
mal/malo(a) bad (weather, news)
maleta f case ; suitcase
maletero m boot (car)

Mallorca f Majorca
malo(a) bad
mañana tomorrow
 mañana f morning
mancha f stain ; mark
mandar por fax to fax
mandíbula f jaw
mando a distancia m remote control
manera f way ; manner
manga f sleeve
manguera f hosepipe
manillar m handlebars
mano f hand
 de segunda mano secondhand
manopla f mitten
 manopla de horno oven gloves
manso(a) tame (animal)
manta f blanket
mantel m tablecloth
mantener to maintain ; to keep
mantequería f dairy products
mantequilla f butter
 mantequilla de cacahuete peanut butter
mantita f picnic rug
manzana f apple ; block (of houses)
manzanilla f camomile tea ; dry sherry
mapa m map
 mapa de carreteras road map
maquillaje m make-up
máquina f machine
 máquina de afeitar razor
 máquina de fotos camera
mar m sea
marca f brand ; make
marcapasos m pacemaker
marcar to dial
 marcar un gol to score a goal
marcha f gear
 marcha atrás reverse gear
marco m picture frame
marea f tide
 marea alta/baja high/low tide
mareado(a) sea sick ; dizzy

margarina f margarine
marido m husband
marioneta f puppet
mariposa f butterfly
mariscos mpl seafood ; shellfish
marisquería f seafood restaurant
mármol m marble
marrón brown
marroquí Moroccan
marroquinería f leather goods

MARTES Tuesday

martillo m hammer

MARZO March

más more ; plus
  más que more than
  más tarde later
masa f pastry (dough)
masculino(a) male
matar to kill
matrícula f car number plate
matrimonio m marriage
máximo m maximum

MAYO May

mayonesa f mayonnaise
mayor parte de most of
mayor que bigger than
mayores de 18 años over-18s
mayúscula f capital letter
mazapán m marzipan
mazo m mallet
mecánico m mechanic
mechero m lighter
medianoche f midnight
medias fpl tights ; stockings
medicina f medicine ; drug
médico(a) m/f doctor
medida f measurement ; size
medio m the middle
medio(a) half
medio(a) half
  media hora half an hour
  media pensión half board

medio hecho(a) medium rare
mediodía : las doce del
  mediodía m midday ; noon
medir to measure
Mediterráneo m Mediterranean
medusa f jellyfish
mejicano(a) m/f Mexican
Méjico m Mexico
mejilla f cheek
mejor best ; better
  mejor que better than
mejorana f marjoram
melocotón m peach
melón m melon
menaje m kitchen utensils
  menaje de hogar household
  goods
mendigo(a) m/f beggar
menestra f vegetable stew
meningitis f meningitis
menor smaller/smallest ; least
Menorca f Minorca
menos minus ; less ; except
  menos que less than
mensaje m message
mensual monthly
menta f mint ; peppermint
mentira f lie (untruth)
menú m menu
  menú del día set menu
mercado m market
mercancías fpl goods
mercería f haberdasher's
merendero m open-air snack bar ;
  picnic area
merienda f afternoon snack ; picnic
mermelada f jam
  mermelada de naranja orange
  marmalade
mes m month
mesa f table
mesón m traditional restaurant
metal metal
metro m metre ; underground ;
  tape measure

m

mezclar to mix
mi my
miel f honey
mientras while

MIÉRCOLES Wednesday

miga f crumb
migraña f migraine
mil thousand
mil millones billion
milagro m miracle
milímetro m millimetre
millón m million
mínimo m minimum
minusválido(a) disabled
minuto m minute
miope short-sighted
mirar to look at ; to watch
misa f mass (in church)
mismo(a) same
mitad f half
mixto(a) mixed

m

mochila f backpack ; rucksack
  mochila portabebés baby sling
moda f fashion
moderno(a) modern
modo m way ; manner
  modo de empleo how to use
mojado(a) wet
mole m black chilli sauce
molestar to disturb
molestia f nuisance ; discomfort
molido(a) ground (coffee beans, etc)
molino m mill
  molino de viento windmill
monasterio m monastery
moneda f currency ; coin
  introduzca monedas insert coins
monedero m purse
monitor(a) de esquí m/f ski
  instructor

m

montaña f mountain
montañismo m mountaineering
montar to ride
  montar a caballo to horse ride

montilla m a sherry-type wine
monumento m monument
moqueta f fitted carpet
mora f mulberry ; blackberry
morado(a) purple
mordedura f bite
morder to bite
moretón m bruise
morir to die
mosca f fly
mosquitera f mosquito net
mostrador m counter ; desk
mostrar to show
moto f moped
  moto acuática jet ski
motocicleta f motorbike
motor m engine ; motor
mozo m luggage porter
muchedumbre f crowd
mucho a lot
mucho(a) a lot (of) ; much
muchos(as) many
muela f tooth
muelle m quay ; pier
muerto(a) dead
muestra f exhibition ; sample
mujer f woman ; wife
multa f fine (to be paid)
mundo m world
muñeca f wrist ; doll
muro m wall
músculo m muscle
museo m museum ; art gallery
música f music
muy very
  muy hecho(a) well done (steak)

N

nacer to be born
nacimiento m birth
nación f nation
nacional national ; domestic (flight)
nacionalidad f nationality

nada nothing
  de nada don't mention it
  nada más nothing else
nadador(a) *m/f* swimmer
nadar to swim
nadie nobody
naipes *mpl* playing cards
naranja *f* orange
naranjada *f* orangeade
nariz *f* nose
nata *f* cream
  nata agria soured cream
  nata batida whipped cream
  nata montada whipped cream
natación *f* swimming
natural natural ; fresh ; plain
naturista *m/f* naturist
navaja *f* pocketknife ; penknife
Navidad *f* Christmas
neblina *f* mist
necesario(a) necessary
necesitar to need ; to require
nectarina *f* nectarine
negarse to refuse
negativo *m* negative *(photo)*
negocios *mpl* business
negro(a) black
neumático *m* tyre
  neumáticos antideslizantes
  snow tyres
nevar to snow
nevera *f* refrigerator
  nevera portátil cool-box
nido *m* nest
niebla *f* fog
nieto(a) *m/f* grandson/daughter
nieve *f* snow
NIF *m* tax number *(of company)*
niña *f* girl ; baby girl
niñera *f* nanny
ningún/ninguno(a) none
niño *m* boy ; baby ; child
  niños children *(infants)*
nivel *m* level ; standard
N° *abbrev. for* **número**

noche *f* night
  esta noche tonight
nochebuena *f* Christmas Eve
nochevieja *f* New Year's Eve
nocivo(a) harmful
nombre *m* name
  nombre de pila first name
norte *m* north
Norteamérica *f* America ; USA
norteamericano(a) American
nosotros(as) we *see* **GRAMMAR**
notaría *f* solicitor's office
notario(a) *m/f* notary ; solicitor
noticias *fpl* news
novela *f* novel
novia *f* girlfriend ; fiancée ; bride

NOVIEMBRE November

novio *m* boyfriend ; fiancé ;
  bridegroom
nube *f* cloud
nublado(a) cloudy
nudo(a) nude
nuestro(a) our
Nueva Zelanda *f* New Zealand
nuevo(a) new
nuez *f* walnut
número *m* number ; size ; issue
  número par even *(number)*
nunca never

O

o or
  o... o... either... or...
obispo *m* bishop
objetivo *m* lens *(on camera)*
objeto *m* object
  objetos de valor valuables
  objetos de regalo gifts
obligatorio(a) compulsory
obra *f* work ; play *(theatre)*
  obra maestra masterpiece
obras *fpl* road works
observar to watch

O

obstruido(a) blocked (pipe)
obtener to get (to obtain)
océano m ocean
ocio m spare time

OCTUBRE October

OCUPADO engaged

oeste m west
oferta f special offer
oficina f office
  Oficina de Correos f Post Office
  oficio m church service ;
  profession
ofrecer to offer
oído m ear
oír to hear
ojo m eye
  ¡ojo! look out!
olas fpl waves (on sea)
olivo m olive tree
olor m smell
oloroso m cream sherry
olvidar to forget
onda f wave
ópera f opera
operación f operation (surgical)
operador(a) m/f operator

OPORTUNIDADES bargains

orden f command
ordenador m computer
  ordenador portátil laptop
oreja f ear
organizar to arrange ; to organize
orilla f shore
orina f urine
oro m gold
oscuro(a) dark ; dim
oso m bear (animal)
ostra f oyster
otoño m autumn ; fall
otro(a) other ; another
  otra vez again
oxígeno m oxygen

P

paciente m/f patient (in hospital)
padrastro m stepfather
padre m father
  padres parents
paella f paella (rice dish)
pagado(a) paid
pagar to pay for ; to pay
  pagar al contado to pay cash
  pagar por separado to pay
  separately
pagaré m IOU
página f page
  página web website
Páginas Amarillas Yellow Pages
pago m payment
  pago por adelantado payment
  in advance

PAGUE EN CAJA please pay
  at cash desk

país m country
paisaje m landscape ; countryside
pájaro m bird
pajita f straw (for drinking)
palabra f word
palacio m palace
palco m box (in theatre)
pálido(a) pale
palillo m toothpick
palo m stick ; mast
  palo de golf golf club
paloma f pigeon
pan m bread ; loaf of bread
  pan de centeno rye bread
  pan integral wholemeal bread
  pan de molde sliced bread
  pan tostado toast
panadería f bakery
pañal m nappy
panecillo m bread roll
paño m flannel ; cloth
pantalla f screen
pantalones mpl trousers

pantalones cortos shorts
pantys mpl tights
pañuelo m handkerchief ; scarf
  pañuelo de papel tissue
papa m pope
papa f potato (Lat. Am.)
papel m paper
  papel higiénico toilet paper
  papeles del coche log book (car)
papelería f stationer's
paquete m packet ; parcel
par even (number)
par m pair
para for; towards
parabrisas fpl windscreen
parachoques m bumper (on car)
parada f stop
parado(a) unemployed
parador m state-run hotel
parafina f paraffin
paraguas m umbrella
parar to stop
parecido(a) a similar to
pared f wall (inside)
pareja f couple (2 people)
parque m park
  parque de atracciones funfair
  parque nacional national park
parquímetro m parking meter
parrilla f grill ; barbecue
  a la parrilla grilled
particular private
partida f game ; departure
  partida de nacimiento f birth
  certificate
partido m match (sport) ; party
  (political)
partir to depart
pasa f raisin ; currant
pasado(a) stale (bread) ; rotten
pasaje m ticket ; fare ; alleyway
pasajero(a) m/f passenger
pasaporte m passport
pasar to happen
pasatiempo m hobby ; pastime

Pascua f Easter
  Pascua de Navidad Christmas
  ¡felices Pascuas! happy
  Christmas
paseo m walk ; avenue ;
  promenade
  Paseo Colón Columbus Avenue
pasillo m corridor ; aisle
paso m step ; pace ; pass (mountain)
  paso de ganado cattle crossing
  paso inferior subway
  paso a nivel level crossing
  paso de peatones pedestrian
  crossing
  paso subterráneo subway
pasta f pastry ; pasta
  pasta de dientes toothpaste
pastel m cake ; pie
  pasteles pastries
pastelería f cakes and pastries ;
  cake shop
pastilla f tablet (medicine) ; pill
  pastilla de jabón bar of soap
pastor(a) shepherd ; minister
patata f potato
  patatas fritas french fries ; crisps
patinaje m skating
patinar to skate
patines mpl skates
  patines en línea rollerblades
pato m duck
pavo m turkey
paz f peace
p. ej. abbrev. for **por ejemplo**
peaje m toll
peatón m/f pedestrian
peces mpl fish
pecho m chest (anat.)
pechuga f breast (poultry)
pedir to ask for ; to order
  pedir prestado to borrow
pegamento m gum ; glue
pegar to stick (on) ; to hit
peine m comb
pelar to peel (fruit)
película f film

p

peligro m danger
  peligro de incendio danger of fire
peligroso(a) dangerous
pelo m hair
pelota f ball ; Basque ball game
  pelota de golf golf ball
  pelota de tenis tennis ball
peluca f wig
peluquería f hairdresser's
pendientes mpl earrings
pene m penis
penicilina f penicillin
pensar to think
pensión f guesthouse
  pensión completa full board
  media pensión half board
pensionista m/f senior citizen
peor worse ; worst
pequeño(a) little ; small ; tiny
pera f pear
percha f coat hanger
perder to lose ; to miss (train, etc)
perdido(a) missing (lost)
perdiz f partridge
perdón m pardon ; sorry
perdonar to forgive
perejil m parsley
perezoso(a) lazy
perfecto(a) perfect
perforar: no perforar do not pierce
perfumería f perfume shop
periódico m newspaper
periodista m/f journalist
perla f pearl
permiso m permission ; pass ; permit ; licence
  permiso de caza hunting permit
  permiso de residencia residence permit
  permiso de trabajo work permit
permitido(a) permitted ; allowed
permitir to allow ; to let
pero but

perro m dog
persiana f blind (for window)
persona f person
personal m staff
pesado(a) heavy ; boring
pesar to weigh
pesca f fishing
pescadería f fishmonger's
pescado m fish
pescador(a) m/f fisherman
pescar to fish
peso m weight ; scales
petirrojo m robin
pez m fish
picado(a) chopped ; minced ; rough (sea) ; stung (by insect)
picadura f insect bite ; sting
picante peppery ; hot ; spicy
picar to itch ; to sting
pie m foot
piedra f stone
piel f fur ; skin ; leather
pierna f leg
pieza f room ; part
  piezas del coche car parts
pijama m pyjamas
pila f battery (radio, etc)
píldora f pill
pileta f sink
  pileta (de natación) swimming pool (Lat. Am.)
pimienta f pepper (spice)
  a la pimienta au poivre
pimiento m pepper (vegetable)
piña f pineapple
pinacoteca f art gallery
pinchar to have a puncture
pinchazo m puncture
pinchos mpl savoury titbits
  pinchos morunos kebabs
pintar to paint
pintura f paint ; painting
pinza f clothes peg
pinzas fpl tweezers
pipa f pipe (smoker's)

pipirrana f tomato/cucumber salad
Pirineos mpl Pyrenees
piruleta f lollipop
pisar to step on ; to tread on
  no pisar el césped keep off grass
piscina f swimming pool
piso m floor ; storey ; flat
  piso deslizante slippery road
pista f track ; court
pistacho m pistachio
pisto m sautéed vegetables
pistola f gun
placa f licence plate
plancha f iron (for clothes)
  a la plancha grilled
planchar to iron
plano m plan ; town map
planta f plant ; floor ; sole (of foot)

PLANTA BAJA ground floor

plata f silver ; money
plátano m banana ; plane tree
platea f stalls (theatre)
plateria f jeweller's
platillo m saucer
platinos mpl points (in car)
plato m plate ; dish (food) ; course
  plato del día dish of the day
  plato principal main course
  plato satélite satellite dish
playa f beach ; seaside
plaza f square (in town)
  plaza de toros bull ring

PLAZAS LIBRES vacancies

plazo m period ; expiry date
plomo m lead (metal)
pluma f feather
pobre poor
poco(a) little
  poco hecho(a) rare (steak)
  un poco de a bit of
pocos(as) (a) few
poder to be able see **GRAMMAR**
podólogo(a) m/f chiropodist
podrido(a) rotten (fruit, etc)

policía f police
policía m/f policeman/woman
  Policía Municipal traffic police
polideportivo m leisure centre
póliza f policy ; certificate
  póliza de seguros insurance
  policy
pollería f poultry shop
pollo m chicken
polo m ice lolly
poltrona f armchair
polvo m powder ; dust
  polvos de talco talcum powder
pomada f ointment
pomelo m grapefruit
ponche m punch
poner to put
  poner en marcha to start (car)
  ponerse en contacto to contact
por by ; per ; through ; about
  por adelantado in advance
  por correo by mail
  por ejemplo for example
  por favor please
porción f portion
porque because
portaequipajes m luggage rack
portero m caretaker ; doorman
portugués(guesa) Portuguese
posible possible
posología f dosage
postal f postcard
postigos mpl shutters
postre m dessert ; sweet
potable drinkable
potaje m stew ; thick soup
pote m stew
potito m baby food
pozo m well (water)
  pozo séptico septic tank
prado m meadow
precio m price ; cost
precioso(a) lovely
precipicio m cliff ; precipice
preciso(a) precise ; necessary

p

preferir to prefer
prefijo m dialling code
pregunta f question
preguntar to ask
premio m prize
prensa f press
preocupado(a) worried
preparado(a) cooked
preparar to prepare ; to cook meal
presa f dam
prescribir to prescribe
presentar to introduce
preservativo m condom
presión f pressure
  presión arterial blood
  pressure
prestar to lend
primavera f spring *(season)*
primer/o(a) first
  primeros auxilios first aid
primo(a) m/f cousin
princesa f princess
principal main
príncipe m prince
principiante m/f beginner
prioridad (de paso) right of way
prismáticos mpl binoculars

PRIVADO private

probadores mpl changing rooms
probar to try ; to taste
probarse to try on *(clothes)*
problema m problem
procedente de... coming from...
productos mpl produce ; products
  productos lácteos dairy produce
profesión f profession ; job
profesor(a) m/f teacher
profundo(a) deep
programa m programme
  programa de ordenador computer program

PROHIBIDO prohibited/no...

prohibido bañarse no bathing

prohibido el paso no entry
prometer to promise
prometido(a) engaged *(to be
married)*
pronóstico m forecast
pronóstico del tiempo m
  weather forecast
pronto soon
pronunciar to pronounce
propiedad f property
propietario(a) m/f owner
propina f tip
propio(a) own
protegido(a) sheltered
provisional temporary
próximo(a) next
público m audience
público(a) public
puchero m cooking pot ; stew
pueblo m village ; country
puente m bridge
puerro m leek
puerta f door ; gate
  cierren la puerta close the door
  puerta de embarque boarding
  gate
  puerta principal front door
puerto m port ; pass *(mountain)*
puesta de sol f sunset
puesta en marcha f starter *(of car)*
puesto que since
pulgada = approx. 2.5 cm inch
pulgar m thumb
pulgas fpl fleas
pulmón m lung
pulpo m octopus
pulsera f bracelet
punto m stitch
punto muerto m neutral *(car)*
puntuación f score *(of match)*
puré m purée
puro m cigar
puro(a) pure

Q

que than ; that
¿qué? what? ; which?
  ¿qué tal? how are you?
quedar to remain ; to be left
  quedar bien to fit *(clothes)*
queja f complaint
quemado(a) burnt *(food)*
quemadura f burn
  quemadura del sol sunburn
quemar to burn
querer to want ; to love *see*
  GRAMMAR
querer decir to mean
querido(a) dear *(on letter)*
queroseno m paraffin
queso m cheese
¿quién? who?
quincena f fortnight
quinientos(as) five hundred
quiosco m kiosk
quiste m cyst
quita-esmalte m nail polish
  remover
quitamanchas m stain remover
quitar to remove
quizás perhaps

R

rabia f rabies
ración f portion
  raciones snacks
radiador m radiator
radio f radio ; spoke *(wheel)*
radiocasete m cassette player
radiografía f X-ray
rallador m cheese grater
rama f branch *(of tree)*
ramo m bunch *(of flowers)*
rápido m express train ; heel bar
rápido(a) quick ; fast
raqueta f racket

rasgar to tear ; to rip
rastrillo m rake
Rastro m flea market
rata f rat
ratero m pickpocket
rato m a while
ratón m mouse
razón f reason
real royal

  REBAJAS sale

recalenatar to overheat
recambio m spare ; refill
recargar to recharge *(battery, etc)*
recepción f reception
recepcionista m/f receptionist
receta f prescription ; recipe
recibir to receive
recibo m receipt
recientemente recently
reclamación f claim ; complaint
reclamar to claim
recoger to collect
recogida f collection
  recogida de equipajes baggage
  reclaim
recomendar to recommend
reconocer to recognize
recordar to remember
recorrido m journey ; route
  de largo recorrido long-distance
recuerdo m souvenir
recuperarse to recover *(from illness)*
red f net
redondo(a) round *(shape)*
reducción f reduction
reducir to reduce
reembolsar to reimburse ; to
  refund
reembolso m refund
refresco m refreshment ; drink
refugio m shelter ; moutain hut
regadera f shower *(Lat. Am.)* ;
  watering can
regalo m gift ; present

179

r

régimen m diet
región f district ; area ; region
registrarse to register (at hotel)
regla f period (menstruation) ; ruler (for measuring)
reina f queen
Reino Unido m United Kingdom
reintegro m withdrawal (from bank account)
reírse to laugh
rejilla f rack (luggage)
relámpago m lightning
rellenar to fill in
reloj m clock ; watch
remar to row (boat)
remitente m/f sender
remolcar to tow
remolque m tow rope ; trailer
RENFE Spanish National Railways
reparación f repair
reparar to repair
repetir to repeat

r **repollo** m cabbage
representante m/f sales rep
repuestos mpl spare parts
resaca f hangover
resbaladizo(a) slippery
resbalarse to slip
rescatar to rescue
reserva f booking(s) ; reservation
reservado(a) reserved
reservar to reserve ; to book
resfriado m cold (illness)
residente m/f resident
resistente a resistant to
  resistente al agua waterproof
  resistente al horno ovenproof
respirar to breathe
responder to answer ; to reply
responsabilidad f responsibility
respuesta f answer

r **restaurante** m restaurant
resto m the rest
retrasado(a) delayed
retraso m delay

sin retraso on schedule
retrato m portrait
retrovisor exterior m wing mirror
reumatismo m rheumatism
reunión f meeting
revelar to develop (photos)
revisar to check
revisión f car service ; inspection
revisor(a) m/f ticket collector
revista f magazine
rey m king
rezar to pray
riada f flash flood
rico(a) rich (person)
rincón m corner
riñón m kidney
riñonera f bumbag
río m river
robar to steal
robo m robbery ; theft
robot m mixer (food processor)
rodaballo m turbot
rodeado(a) de surrounded by
rodilla f knee
rodillo m rolling pin
rojo(a) red
románico(a) Romanesque
romántico(a) romantic
romería f pilgrimage
romper to break ; to tear
ron m rum
roncar to snore
ropa f clothes
  ropa interior underwear
  ropa de cama bed clothes
ropero m wardrobe
rosa f rose
rosa pink
rosado m rosé
roto(a) broken
rotonda f roundabout (traffic)
rotulador m felt-tip pen
rubeola f rubella ; German measles
rubio(a) blond ; fair haired

rueda f wheel
  rueda de repuesto spare tyre
  rueda pinchada flat tyre
ruido m noise
ruinas fpl ruins
ruta turística f tourist route

S

SA abbrev. for **Sociedad Anónima**

SÁBADO Saturday

sábana f sheet (bed)
saber to know (facts) ; to know how
sabor m taste ; flavour
sacacorchos m corkscrew
sacar to take out (of bag, etc)
sacarina f saccharin
saco m sack
  saco de dormir sleeping bag
sagrado(a) holy
sal f salt
  sin sal unsalted
sala f hall ; hospital ward
  sala de conciertos concert hall
  sala de embarque departure
  lounge
  sala de espera waiting room
salado(a) savoury ; salty
salario m wage
salchicha f sausage
saldo m balance of account
saldos mpl sales

SALIDA exit/departure

  salida de incendios fire escape
  salida del sol sunrise
salir to go out ; to come out
salmón m salmon
  salmón ahumado smoked
  salmon
salsa f gravy ; sauce ; dressing
saltar to jump
salteado(a) sauté, sautéed
salud f health
  ¡salud! cheers!

salvar to save (life)
salvaslips m panty liner
salvavidas m lifebelt
salvia f sage (herb)
sandalias fpl sandals
sandía f watermelon
sangrar to bleed
sangría f red wine and fruit punch
santo(a) saint ; holy
sarampión m measles
sarpullido m skin rash
sartén m frying pan
sastrería f tailor's
secado a mano m blow-dry
secador de pelo m hairdryer
secadora f dryer (spin, tumble)
secar to dry
seco(a) dry ; dried (fruit, beans)
secretario(a) m/f secretary
seda f silk
  seda dental dental floss
seguida: en seguida straight away
seguido(a) continuous
  todo seguido straight on
seguir to continue ; to follow
según according to
segundo m second (time)
segundo(a) second
  de segunda mano secondhand
seguramente probably
seguridad f reliability; safety
seguro m insurance
  seguro de vida life insurance
  seguro del coche car insurance
  seguro médico medical insurance
seguro(a) safe ; certain
sello m stamp (postage)
semáforo m traffic lights
semana f week
  Semana Santa Holy Week ;
  Easter
semanal weekly
semilla f seed ; pip
señal f sign ; signal ; road sign
sencillo(a) simple ; single (ticket)

181

S

señor m gentleman
  Señor (Sr.) Mr. ; sir
señora f lady
  Señora (Sra.) Mrs. ; Ms ; Madam
señorita f Miss
  Señorita (Srta.)... Miss...
sentarse to sit
sentir to feel
separado(a) separated *(couple)*
septentrional northern

SEPTIEMBRE September

sequía f drought
ser to be *see* **GRAMMAR**
seropositivo(a) HIV positive
serpiente snake
servicio m service ; service charge
  servicio incluido service included
  área de servicios service area
  servicios de urgencia emergency services

SERVICIOS toilets

servilleta f serviette ; napkin
servir to serve
sesión f performance ; screening
  sesión de noche late night performance
  sesión numerada seats bookable in advance
  sesión de tarde eve performance
sesos mpl brains
seta f mushroom
sexo m sex ; gender
sí yes
sida m AIDS
sidra f cider
siempre always
siento: lo siento I'm sorry
sierra f mountain range ; saw
siga follow
  siga adelante carry on
  siga derecho keep straight on
siglo m century
siguiente following ; next
silencio m silence

silla f chair ; seat
  silla de niño pushchair
  silla de ruedas wheelchair
sillón m armchair
simpático(a) nice ; kind
sin without
  sin plomo lead-free
síntoma m symptom

SÍRVASE VD. MISMO serve yourself

sistema m system
sitio m place ; space ; position
slip m pants ; briefs
sobre on ; upon ; about ; on top of
sobre m envelope
  sobre acolchado padded envelope
sobrecarga f surcharge
sobrecargar to overload
sobredosis f overdose
sobrino(a) m/f nephew/niece
sobrio(a) sober
sociedad f society
  Sociedad Anónima Ltd. ; plc
socio m member ; partner
socorrista m lifeguard
¡socorro! help!
soja f soya
sol m sun ; sunshine
solamente only
soldado m soldier
solicitar to request
solitario m patience *(cardgame)*
solo(a) lone ; lonely
sólo only
solomillo m sirloin
soltero m bachelor
soltero(a) single *(unmarried)*
sombra f shade ; shadow
  sombra de ojos eye shadow
sombrero m hat
sombrilla f sunshade ; parasol
somnífero m sleeping pill

sonido m sound
sonreír to smile
sonrisa f smile
sopa f soup
sordo(a) deaf
sorpresa f surprise

SÓTANO for sale

soya f soya
Sr. abbrev. for **señor**
Sra. abbrev. for **señora**
Srta. abbrev. for **señorita**
stop stop (sign)
su his/her/their/your
suavizante m hair conditioner
submarinismo m scuba diving
subterráneo(a) underground
subtítulo m subtitle
sucio(a) dirty
sucursal f branch (of bank, etc)
sudadera f sweatshirt
sudar to sweat
suegro(a) m/f mother/
  father-in-law
suela f sole (of foot, shoe)
sueldo m wage
suelo m soil ; ground ; floor
suelto m loose change (money)
sueño m dream
suerte f luck
  ¡buena suerte! good luck!
Suiza f Switzerland
suizo(a) Swiss
sujetador m bra
superior higher
supermercado m supermarket
supositorio m suppository
sur m south
surf m surfing
surtidor m petrol pump
sus his/her/their

T

tabaco m tobacco
tabla f board
  tabla de cortar chopping board
  tabla de planchar ironing board
  tabla de surf surf board
tablao flamenco m Flamenco show
tableta f tablet ; bar (chocolate)
taco m stuffed tortilla
tacón m heel (shoe)
taladradora f drill (tool)
talco m talc
TALGO m Intercity train
talla f size
tallarines mpl noodles ; tagliatelle
taller m garage for repairs
talón m heel ; counterfoil ; stub
  talón bancario cheque
talonarlo m cheque book
también as well ; also ; too
tampoco neither
tampones mpl tampons
tapa f lid
tapas fpl appetizers
tapón cap (for sink)

TAQUILLA ticket office

tarde f evening ; afternoon
  de la tarde pm
tarde late
tarifa f price ; rate
  tarifa baja cheap rate
  tarifa máxima peak rate
tarjeta f card
  tarjeta bancaria banker's card
  tarjeta de crédito credit card
  tarjeta de donante donor card
  tarjeta de embarque boarding
  pass
  tarjeta de visita business card
  tarjeta telefónica phonecard
  tarjeta verde green card
tarro m jar ; pot
tarta f cake ; tart

t

tasca f bar ; cheap restaurant
taxista m/f taxi driver
taza f cup
tazón bowl (for soup, etc)
té m tea
teatro m theatre
techo m ceiling
  techo solar sunroof
tejado m roof
tela f material ; fabric
  tela impermeable groundsheet
telaraña f web (spider)
teleférico m cablecar
telefonear to call ; to phone
telefonista m/f telephonist
teléfono m phone ; telephone
  teléfono móbil mobile phone
  teléfono público payphone
telegrama m telegram
telesilla m ski lift ; chairlift
telesquí m ski lift
televisión f television
televisor m television set
télex m telex
temperatura f temperature
templo m temple
temporada f season
  temporada alta high season
temporal m storm
temporizador m timer (on cooker)
temprano(a) early
tendedero m clothes line
tenedor m fork (for eating)
tener to have see **GRAMMAR**
  tener 'overbooking' to be
  overbooked
  tener miedo de to be afraid of
  tener morriña to be homesick
  tener que to have to
  tener razón to be right
  tener suerte to be lucky
  tener fiebre to have a
  temperature
tentempié m snack
tequila f tequila
tercero(a) third

terciopelo m velvet
termo m flask (thermos)
termómetro m thermometer
ternera f veal
terraza f terrace
terremoto m earthquake
terreno m land
terrorista m/f terrorist
testículos mpl testicles
tetera f teapot
tetina f teat (on baby's bottle)
tía f aunt
tiempo m time ; weather
tienda f store ; shop ; tent
  tienda de modas clothes shop
tierra f earth
tijeras fpl scissors
  tijeras de uñas nail scissors
timbre m doorbell ; official stamp
tímido(a) shy
timón m rudder
tinta f ink
tinte m dye
  tinte de pelo hair dye
tinto m red wine
tintorería f dry-cleaner's
tío m uncle
típico(a) typical
tipo m sort
  tipo de cambio exchange rate
tíquet m ticket

TIRAD pull

tirador m handle
tirar to throw (away) ; to pull
  para tirar disposable
tiritas® fpl elastoplast
toalla f towel
tobillo m ankle
tocar to touch ; to play (instrument)

NO TOCAR do not touch

tocino m bacon
todo(a) all
  todo everything

184

todo el mundo everyone
todo incluido all inclusive
tomar to take ; to have *(food/drink)*
  tomar el sol to sunbathe
tomate m tomato
tomillo m thyme
tónica f tonic water
tono m tone
  tono de marcar dialling tone
tonto(a) stupid
toquen: no toquen do not touch
torcedura f sprain
torero m bullfighter
tormenta f thunderstorm
tornillo m screw
toro m bull
torre f tower
torta f cake
tortilla f omelette ; thin maize
  pancake
tos f cough
toser to cough
tostada f toast
trabajar to work *(person)*
trabajo m work
tradicional traditional
traducción f translation
traducir to translate
traer to fetch ; to bring
tráfico m traffic
tragar to swallow
traje m suit ; outfit
  traje de baño swimsuit
  traje de bucear wetsuit
  traje de etiqueta evening dress
  (man's)
  traje de noche evening dress
  (woman's)
trampolín m diving board
tranquilo(a) calm ; quiet
tranquilizante m tranquilliser
transbordador m car ferry
transbordo m transfer
tranvía m tram ; short-distance
  train

trapo m cloth *(for cleaning, etc)*
tras after ; behind
trastorno estomacal m stomach
  upset
tratar con cuidado handle with
  care
travesía f crossing
tren m train
triángulo señalizador m warning
  triangle
triste sad
trozo m piece
trucha f trout
trueno m thunder
trufa f truffle
tú your *(sing. with friends)*
tubería f pipe *(drain, etc)*
tubo de escape m exhaust pipe
tumbarse to lie down
tumbona f deckchair
túnel m tunnel
turista m/f tourist
turístico(a) tourist
turno m turn
  espere su turno wait your turn
turrón m nougat
TVE abbrev. for Televisión
  Española

U

Ud(s) see **usted(es)**
úlcera f ulcer *(stomach)*
últimamente lately
último(a) last
ultracongelador m deep freeze
ultramarinos m grocery shop
un(a) a/an
uña f nail *(finger, toe)*
ungüento m ointment
únicamente only
unidad f unit
Unión Europea European Union
universidad f university
unos(as) some

URGENCIAS casualty department

urgente urgent ; express
usar to use
uso m use ; custom
  uso externo/tópico for external
  use only
usted you *(polite sing.)* see
  GRAMMAR
ustedes you *(polite plural)*
útil useful
utilizar to use
uva f grape
  uvas verdes/negras
  green/black grapes
UVI f intensive care unit

V

vaca f cow
vacaciones fpl holiday
  vacaciones de verano summer
  holidays
vacío(a) empty
vacuna f vaccination
vagina f vagina
vagón m railway carriage
vale OK
vale... worth: it's worth...
vale m token ; voucher
válido(a) valid *(ticket, licence, etc)*
valle m valley
valor m value
válvula f valve
vapor m steam
  al vapor steamed
vaqueros mpl jeans
variado(a) assorted ; mixed
varios(as) several
vasco(a) Basque
vaso m glass *(for drinking)*
Vd(s) abbrev. for **usted(es)**
veces fpl times
vecino(a) neighbour
vegetaliano(a) m/f vegan

vegetariano(a) m/f vegetarian
vehículo m vehicle
vela f candle ; sail ; sailing
velocidad f speed
  velocidad limitada speed limit
  velocidad máxima speed limit
velocímetro m speedometer
vena f vein
venda f bandage
vendedor(a) m/f salesman/woman
vender to sell

SE VENDE for sale

veneno m poison
venenoso(a) poisonous
venir to come
venta f sale; country inn
ventana f window
ventanilla f window *(in car, train)*
ventilador m fan *(electric)*
ver to see ; to watch
verano m summer
verdad f truth
  ¿de verdad? really?
verdadero(a) true ; genuine
verde green
verdulería f greengrocer's
verduras fpl vegetables
vereda f footpath *(in the country)*
verificar to check
versión f version
  versión original original version
vespa f motor scooter
vestido m dress
  vestir de etiqueta formal dress
vestirse to dress *(to get dressed)*
veterinario(a) m/f vet
vez f time
vía f track ; rails ; platform
  por vía oral/bucal orally
viajar to travel
viaje m journey ; trip
  viaje de negocios business trip
  viaje organizado package tour
viajero m traveller

víbora f adder ; viper
vida f life
vídeo m video ; video recorder
videocámara f camcorder
videojuego m video game
vidriera f stained-glass window
vidrio m glass (substance)
vieira f scallop
viejo(a) old
viento m wind

VIERNES Friday

viernes santo Good Friday
viña; vineyard
vinagre m vinegar
vinagreta f vinaigrette (dressing)
vino m wine
  vino blanco white wine
  vino rosado rosé wine
  vino seco dry wine
  vino tinto red wine
violación f rape
violar to rape
violeta f violet (flower)
virus m virus
  virus del sida HIV
visa f visa
visita f visit
visitar to visit
víspera f eve
vista f view
vitrina f shop window (Lat. Am.)
viudo(a) m/f widow/widower
vivir to live
VO (versión original) undubbed version (of film)
volante m steering wheel
volar to fly
volcán m volcano

voleibol m volleyball
voltaje m voltage
volumen m volume
volver to come/go back ; to return
vomitar to vomit
vosotros you (plural with friends)
voz f voice
vuelo m flight
vuelta f turn ; return ; change (money)

W

wáter m lavatory ; toilet

Y

y and
yate m yacht
yerno m son-in-law
yo I ; me see **GRAMMAR**
yogur m yoghurt
  yogur natural plain yoghurt

Z

zanahoria f carrot
zapatería f shoe shop
zapatillas fpl slippers
  zapatillas de deporte trainers
zapato m shoe
zarzuela f Spanish light opera; casserole
zona f zone
  zona azul controlled parking area
  zona de descanso layby
  zona restringida restricted area
zorro m fox
zumo m juice

NOUNS

Unlike English, Spanish nouns have a gender: they are either *masculine* (**el**) or *feminine* (**la**). Therefore words for *the* and *a(n)* must agree with the noun they accompany – whether *masculine*, *feminine* or *plural*:

	masc.	*fem.*	*plural*
the	**el gato**	**la plaza**	**los gatos, las plazas**
a, an	**un gato**	**una plaza**	**unos gatos**, **unas plazas**

The ending of the noun will usually indicate whether it is *masculine* or *feminine*:

-o or **-or** are generally *masculine*

-a, **-dad**, **-ión**, **-tud**, **-umbre** are generally *feminine*

NOTE: *feminine* nouns beginning with a stressed **a-** or **ha-** take the *masculine* article **el**, though the noun is still *feminine*.

FORMATION OF PLURALS

The articles **el** and **la** become **los** and **las** in the plural. Nouns ending with a vowel become plural by adding **s**:

> **el gato → los gatos**
> **la plaza → las plazas**
> **la calle → las calles**

Where the noun ends in a consonant, then **-es** is added:

> **el color → los colores**
> **la ciudad → las ciudades**

Nouns ending in **-z** change their ending to **-ces** in the plural.

> **el lápiz → los lápices**
> **la voz → las voces**

ADJECTIVES

Adjectives normally follow the noun they describe in Spanish,
e.g. **la manzana roja** (**the red apple**)

Some common exceptions which go before the noun are:

buen good; **gran** great; **ningún** no, not any; **mucho** much, many; **poco** little, few; **primer** first; **tanto** so much, so many.
e.g. **el último tren** (the last train)

Spanish adjectives also reflect the gender of the noun they describe. To make an adjective *feminine*, the *masculine* **-o** ending is changed to **-a** ; and the endings **-án**, **-ón**, **-or**, **-és** change to **-ana**, **-ona**, **-ora**, **-esa**:

masc. **el libro rojo**	*fem.* **la manzana roja**
(the red book)	(the red apple)

masc. **el hombre hablador**	*fem.* **la mujer habladora**
(the talkative man)	(the talkative woman)

To make an adjective plural an **-s** is added to the singular form if it ends in a vowel. If the adjective ends in a consonant, **-es** is added:

masc. **los libros rojos**	*fem.* **las manzanas rojas**
(the red books)	(the red apples)
masc. **los hombres habladores**	*fem* **las mujeres habladoras**
(the talkative men)	(the talkative women)

MY, YOUR, HIS, HER...

These words also depend on the gender and number of the noun they accompany and not on the sex of the 'owner'.

	with masc. sing. noun	with fem sing. noun	with plural nouns
my	**mi**	**mi**	**mis**
your *(familiar sing.)*	**tu**	**tu**	**tus**
your *(polite sing.)*	**su**	**su**	**sus**
his/her/its	**su**	**su**	**sus**
our	**nuestro**	**nuestra**	**nuestros/nuestras**
your *(familiar pl.)*	**vuestro**	**vuestra**	**vuestros/vuestras**
their	**su**	**su**	**sus**
your *(polite pl.)*	**su**	**su**	**sus**

There is no distinction between **his** and **her** in Spanish: **su billete** can mean either **his** or **her ticket**.

PRONOUNS

subject		*object*	
I	**yo**	me	**me**
you *(familiar sing.)*	**tú**	you	**te**
you *(polite sing.)*	**usted (Vd.)**	you	**le**
he/it	**él**	him/it	**le, lo**
she/it	**ella**	her/it	**le, la**
we	**nosotros**	us	**nos**
you *(familiar pl.)*	**vosotros**	you	**os**
you *(polite pl.)*	**ustedes (Vds.)**	you	**les**
they *(masc.)*	**ellos**	them	**les, los**
they *(fem.)*	**ellas**	them	**les, las**

Subject pronouns (**I**, **you**, **he**, etc.) are generally omitted in Spanish, since the verb ending distinguishes the subject:

hab<u>lo</u>	<u>I</u> speak
hab<u>lamos</u>	<u>we</u> speak

However, they are used for emphasis or to avoid confusion:

> **yo voy a Mallorca y él va a Alicante**
> I am going to Mallorca and he is going to Alicante

Object pronouns are placed before the verb in Spanish:

la veo	I see her
los conocemos	we know them

However, in commands or requests they follow the verb:

¡ayúdame!	help me!
escúchale	listen to him

except when they are expressed in the negative:

¡no me ayudes!	don't help me
no le escuches	don't listen to him

The object pronouns shown above can be used to mean to me, to us, etc., but to him/to her is **le** and to them is **les**. If **le** and **les** occur in combinations with **lo/la/las/los** then **le/les** change to **se**, e.g. **se lo doy** (I give it to him).

VERBS

There are three main patterns of endings for Spanish verbs – those ending -**ar**, -**er** and -**ir** in the dictionary.

	CANTAR	**TO SING**
	canto	I sing
	cantas	you sing
(usted)	**canta**	(s)he sings/you sing
	cantamos	we sing
	cantáis	you sing
(ustedes)	**cantan**	they sing/you sing

	VIVIR	**TO LIVE**
	vivo	I live
	vives	you live
(usted)	**vive**	(s)he lives/you live
	vivimos	we live
	vivís	you live
(ustedes)	**viven**	they live/you live

	COMER	**TO EAT**
	como	I eat
	comes	you eat
(usted)	**come**	(s)he eats/you eat
	comemos	we eat
	coméis	you eat
(ustedes)	**comen**	they eat/you eat

Like French, in Spanish there are two ways of addressing people: the polite form (for people you don't know well or who are older) and the familiar form (for friends, family and children). The polite you is **usted** in the singular, and **ustedes** in the plural. You can see from above that **usted** uses the same verb ending as for he and she; **ustedes** the same ending as for they. Often the words **usted** and **ustedes** are omitted, but the verb ending itself indicates that you are using the polite form. The informal words for you are **tú** (singular) and **vosotros** (plural).

THE VERB 'TO BE'

There are two different Spanish verbs for **to be** – **ser** and **estar**.

Ser is used to describe a permanent state:

soy inglés	I am English
es una playa	it is a beach

Estar is used to describe a temporary state or where something is located:

¿cómo está?	how are you?
¿dónde está la playa?	where is the beach?

	SER	ESTAR	TO BE
	soy	**estoy**	I am
	eres	**estás**	you are
(usted)	**es**	**está**	(s)he is/you are
	somos	**estamos**	we are
	sois	**estáis**	you are
(ustedes)	**son**	**están**	they are/you are

Other common irregular verbs include:

	TENER	TO HAVE	IR	TO GO
	tengo	I have	**voy**	I go
	tienes	you have	**vas**	you go
(usted)	**tiene**	(s)he has	**va**	(s)he goes
	tenemos	we have	**vamos**	we go
	tenéis	you have	**vais**	you go
(ustedes)	**tienen**	they have	**van**	they go

	PODER	TO BE ABLE	QUERER	TO WANT
	puedo	I can	**quiero**	I want
	puedes	you can	**quieres**	you want
(usted)	**puede**	(s)he can	**quiere**	(s)he wants
	podemos	we can	**queremos**	we want
	podéis	you can	**queréis**	you want
(ustedes)	**pueden**	they can	**quieren**	they want

	HACER	TO DO	VENIR	TO COME
	hago	I do	**vengo**	I come
	haces	you do	**vienes**	you come
(usted)	**hace**	(s)he does	**viene**	(s)he comes
	hacemos	we do	**venimos**	we come
	hacéis	you do	**venís**	you come
(ustedes)	**hacen**	they do	**vienen**	they come

PAST TENSE

To form the past tense, for example: I gave/I have given, I finished/I have finished, combine the present tense of the verb **haber** – to have with the past participle of the verb (**cantado, comido, vivido**):

	HABER	TO HAVE
	he	I have
	has	you have
(usted)	**ha**	(s)he has/you have
	hemos	we have
	habéis	you have
(ustedes)	**han**	they have/you have
e.g.	**he cantado**	I sang/I have sung
	ha comido	he ate/he has eaten
	hemos vivido	we lived/we have lived

To form a negative **no** is placed before all of the verb:

e.g.	**no he cantado**	I haven't sung
	no ha comido	he hasn't eaten
	no hemos vivido	we haven't lived